PRAISE FOR NICK RENNISON

'A delightful book... Intelligent and lively'
– *SCOTSMAN*

'Entertaining and thoroughly readable canter through the
events of a century ago... Fascinating' – *OBSERVER*

'In crisp and evocative snatches, Rennison gives
monthly summaries of global events, domestic episodes,
newspaper sensations, sporting triumphs and cultural
acclaim during 1922' – *SPECTATOR*

'A revealing, kaleidoscopic snapshot of the most
important events of a century ago... Rennison succinctly
and vividly captures the major upheavals of 1922'
– *SUNDAY BUSINESS POST*

'A fast moving and extremely readable book'
– *ALL ABOUT HISTORY*

'An enjoyable biography of an important year that serves
as another reminder of how much history just twelve
months can contain' – *FOREWORD*

'Hugely enjoyable' – *TIMES LITERARY
SUPPLEMENT*

'Vivid, month-by-month snapshots explore the drama
and diversity of 1922' – *CHOICE*

T0191130

ALSO BY NICK RENNISON

SCENES FROM A YEAR OF CRISIS

NICK RENNISON

Oldcastle Books

This paperback edition first published in 2024
by Oldcastle Books Ltd,
Harpenden, UK

oldcastlebooks.co.uk
@OldcastleBooks

© Nick Rennison, 2023

The right of Nick Rennison to be identified as the author of this
work has been asserted in accordance with the Copyright,
Designs and Patents Act 1988.

All rights reserved. No part of this book may be reproduced, stored
in or introduced into a retrieval system, or transmitted, in any form
or by any means (electronic, mechanical, photocopying, recording or
otherwise) without the written permission of the publishers.

Any person who does any unauthorised act in relation to this publication
may be liable to criminal prosecution and civil claims for damages.

A CIP catalogue record for this book is available from the British Library.

ISBN
978-0-85730-582-4 (Hardcover)
978-0-85730-581-7 (Paperback)
978-0-85730-583-1 (Ebook)

2 4 6 8 10 9 7 5 3 1

Typeset in 11.1pt Goudy Old Style
by Avocet Typeset, Bideford, Devon, EX39 2BP
Printed and bound in Great Britain by Clays Ltd, Elcograf S.p.A.

MIX
Paper | Supporting
responsible forestry
FSC® C018072

To David Jones, a great friend for nearly 50 years
whom I first met in... 1974

'To those of us who lived through that era of polyester, platform shoes and power cuts, one thing seemed certain: no one would ever wish to revisit it' – Francis Wheen

'Hindsight is a great simplifier, and the seventies as an era has been simplified more than most' – Andy Beckett

Contents

SCENES FROM A YEAR OF CRISIS

Introduction

The 1970s is not a decade that has enjoyed a very good press, particularly in Britain. It's been called 'the decade that taste forgot' so often that the phrase has become a cliché. 'If the 1960s were a wild weekend and the 1980s a hectic day at the office,' Francis Wheen wrote in his hugely entertaining book, *Strange Days Indeed*, 'the 1970s were a long Sunday evening in winter, with cold leftovers for supper and a power cut expected at any moment.' Yet the decade, viewed with the hindsight of half a century, holds plenty of interest, as I hope this book will show.

An argument can be made for 1976 as its pivotal year. Some might claim that the real turning point, particularly in Britain, came right at its end in 1979. However, 1974 seems to me the one year in the 1970s which best exemplifies the decade. According to the journalist and historian Andy Beckett, this was 'the apocalyptic year of the British seventies'. It was also a year in which huge changes took place around the world. On both sides of the Atlantic, major political figures left the scene, either through resignation or electoral defeat. Leaders of nations died. Regimes crumbled that had lasted decades. Portugal's Carnation Revolution saw the end of a dictatorship that had come to power in the 1930s; in Ethiopia, an emperor who had acceded to the throne in the same decade was toppled from it. Terrorism and the pursuit of political ends through violence became ever more commonplace. The year saw a sustained bombing campaign by the Provisional IRA in both Northern Ireland and on the British mainland; Palestinian terrorists killed more than thirty people, including many children, in the town of Ma'alot; Basque separatists blew up a café in central Madrid.

Sport's growing cultural importance is reflected in the number of entries devoted to it in this book. Football had not yet achieved the kind of worldwide all-pervasiveness (and enormous financial clout) it has today but it was well on the way. The 1974 World Cup attracted huge TV audiences. In Britain, rugby and cricket arguably had greater prominence than they do now and major tours by British teams, well remembered fifty years later, took place in both sports. Tennis saw the arrival of new young talents.

In America, movies were undergoing the renaissance known as 'New Hollywood' in which great directors such as Scorsese, Spielberg and Coppola were making their mark. Popular music was arguably at a low point but the first stirrings of the punk revolution to come could be heard in New York clubs. And a Swedish band that were to become a phenomenon won the Eurovision Song Contest.

1922, the subject of my last book, was not within living memory, except perhaps for a handful of super-centenarians around the world. 1974 most definitely is. Indeed, it is in *my* living memory. That year, I celebrated my nineteenth birthday and left home to enjoy my first term at college. It has been an interesting experience to revisit events of 1974, some of which remain vivid in my mind. I can recall working in a bookshop at the time of the three-day week when the lights went out to be replaced by oil lamps and older members of staff reminisced about wartime power cuts and shortages. I remember watching the World Cup on TV and marvelling at the 'total football' played by the Dutch team. I remember listening to Bowie's *Diamond Dogs* on a rackety old record player in my cousin's bedroom. I can recollect the media furore that surrounded the disappearances of Lord Lucan and John Stonehouse. Other events seemed to have made no mark at all. Did I ever know at the time about Philippe Petit's high-wire walk in New York? Or the prison siege at Huntsville, Texas? Or the train disaster that killed dozens and dozens of people in Zagreb? If I did, I had long since expunged them from my memory before I began the reading for this book.

Reading about and remembering the events of 1974, the year can sometimes seem as if it is far further back in history than a mere fifty years. The famous LP Hartley quote about the past being a foreign country where they do things differently comes readily to mind. Yet at other times, my greatest feeling was one of familiarity. Much of what happened then has echoes now. Like *1922*, this book is a collection of snapshots from the past which I hope readers will find both enlightening and entertaining.

January

New Year's Day becomes a bank holiday. The three-day week begins in Britain. Muhammad Ali and Joe Frazier face one another in the second of their three heavyweight fights. The Commonwealth Games opens in Christchurch, New Zealand. In North Africa, the Djerba Declaration suggests that Tunisia and Libya might become one state – The Arab Islamic Republic. In the USA, Sam Goldwyn, one of Hollywood's most eccentric but successful producers, dies.

New Year's Day

In 1974, the New Year in the UK began with an extra holiday. Most people probably assume that New Year's Day had been a British public holiday ever since bank holidays were first introduced in the nineteenth century. In fact, it was only in Scotland that 1 January officially became a holiday in 1871. The rest of the country had to wait more than a century. (Many people, recovering from over-exuberant celebrations the night before, had unofficially decided it was a day of rest for many years.) The prime minister, Ted Heath, included plans for the extra holiday amidst a whole host of other measures in a televised press conference to announce the third phase of the government's prices and incomes policy on 8 October 1973. Amidst all the less than cheering news about the state of the economy, he may have felt the need to throw in something to please his listeners. The announcement of a New Year's Day bank holiday, which had been proposed in a private member's bill two years earlier and rejected, must have seemed just the ticket. Later that same month a Royal Proclamation ('We... do hereby appoint New Year's Day in the year 1974 to be, in England and Wales and Northern Ireland a bank holiday...') confirmed his statement. Scotland, where the day after Hogmanay had long been a holiday, received a further day for rest and recuperation. As if to prove that it is impossible to please all the people all the time, even when providing them with an extra day's holiday, the Tory MP Richard Hornby wrote a letter to the *Times*, published a week into the New Year, bemoaning the fact that all cultural venues had chosen to shut on 1 January. It's safe to assume that he was in a small minority in not welcoming the new bank holiday.

Ali v. Frazier

Muhammad Ali always referred to himself as 'The Greatest' and plenty of boxing aficionados would agree with him. In proof of their claim that he was the greatest of all heavyweight champions, his fans can point to the years of his prime when he defeated Sonny Liston to take the world title for the first time and then defended it against a succession of fighters. They can also cite his achievements in 1974 when he fought bouts against, arguably, the two best boxers he ever faced and beat them both.

The first fight took place at Madison Square Garden in New York on 28 January and was against 'Smokin' Joe' Frazier. It was the second time that the two boxers had faced one another in the ring. The previous bout, which had been in the same venue nearly three years before, had been nicknamed 'The Fight of the Century'. Frazier had won a unanimous decision on points, inflicting on Ali the first defeat of his professional career and retaining the world titles Smokin' Joe had won earlier that same year. Neither man was now champion, Frazier having lost his titles the previous year when George Foreman despatched him in two rounds in a contest in Kingston, Jamaica. In many ways it was a grudge match. Ali wanted revenge for his defeat; Frazier wanted to prove that his victory in March 1971 had been no fluke.

Tension between the two fighters was already high before they even stepped into the ring. Five days earlier, during a joint appearance in a TV studio, Ali had called Frazier 'ignorant'. Justifiably indignant, Frazier stood menacingly over his seated opponent, shouting, 'Why you call me ignorant? How am I ignorant?' The confrontation had developed into fisticuffs in front of the TV cameras. Both men were later fined for 'deplorable conduct demeaning to boxing'.

After they entered the ring in Madison Square Garden, Ali started the fight as if he meant to bring it to an end as quickly as possible. He nearly did. In the second round, Frazier took a right punch which left him wobbling and in difficulty. The contest might have finished at that point. Frazier retreated to the ropes and Ali moved in for the kill but the referee, Tony Perez, thinking he had heard the bell to end the round, stepped between them. In fact, the bell had malfunctioned and the round went on but Frazier had been granted a precious few extra seconds in which to recover.

As the fight went on, it clearly demonstrated the contrasting styles of the two boxers. Ali, tall and elegant, circled the ring, throwing combinations of punches in quick succession and then holding on to his opponent when he grew tired. (In fact, Ali held on so often that Frazier's trainer, Eddie Futch, complained to the referee, saying 'You gotta stop this!'. The referee told Futch, quite rightly, that clinging to your opponent was allowed. It was holding on and punching at the same time that was illegal and Ali was not doing that.) Frazier, four inches shorter and barrel-chested, moved relentlessly forward, struggling to get under Ali's longer reach and land the kind of knockout left hook that had won him their first fight. At the end of the 12 rounds, all three judges gave the fight to Ali, although one of them – Tony Perez, the referee – saw it as a very close contest, marking six rounds for Ali against five for Frazier with one drawn. 'In the end, it was a unanimous decision for Ali,' one boxing journalist, Mark Kram, wrote, 'ring generalship over a one-man army fighting a war of attrition.' The third and final meeting between the two fighters, the famous 'Thrilla in Manila', took place the following year. Ali was declared the winner again when Frazier's team conceded the bout in the 14th round.

Three-Day Week

Britain began 1974 with severe restrictions on the use of electricity. Ted Heath's Tory government had been growing ever more concerned about the state of the country's economy for many months. One of the chief worries was the power supply. The oil crisis in the Middle East and the threat of another miners' strike to follow that of 1972 were concentrating minds. When the National Union of Miners, the NUM, decided upon a ban on overtime in support of their wage claims and other unions made clear their support for the miners, fears began to grow that coal supplies might run out. In the 1970s, most of the nation's electricity was supplied by coal-burning power stations. The government felt they had no option but to take drastic action.

Some restrictions had come into force nearly two months earlier. A fifth state of emergency in three years had been announced in the House of Commons in the middle of November 1973. Electric floodlighting and advertising had been banned; public offices were told to cut energy consumption by a tenth; TV companies were obliged to cease broadcasting at half past ten. Government adverts began to appear in the newspapers exhorting people to leave their cars at home at weekends and, if they must drive, to keep below 50mph in order to conserve fuel. Those charged with providing the country's energy requirements were growing desperate. 'The choice is stark,' the deputy chairman of the Electricity Council told an American journalist. 'Either the public cooperates or complete cities could lose their supply of electricity at a stroke. It could even happen before Christmas.'

The public did respond to all the calls for more careful consumption but it was not enough. The government decided that more needed to be done. In December 1973, Heath, looking visibly exhausted – he had barely slept in four days – appeared on the nation's TV screens to deliver the bad news. He pulled few punches. 'We shall have a harder Christmas than we have known since the war', he said. 'We shall have to postpone some of the hopes and aims we have set ourselves for expansion and for our standard of living.' He appealed for people to put aside their differences. 'We must close our ranks so that we can deal together with the difficulties which come to us.' And he announced that, beginning at midnight on New Year's Eve 1973, electricity was, in effect, rationed. Commercial consumption was restricted to three consecutive days in the week and shops, unless they were deemed essential, had to choose either mornings or afternoons to switch on the lights. According to one newspaper report, government ministers were secretly even concerned that a two-day week might have to be introduced.

As the lights went out across the country, some people were sympathetic to the government's dilemmas and difficult choices. Others most definitely were not. 'Dictator Heath and his £10,000-plus a year henchmen have imposed a three-day working week,' one correspondent to the *Times* wrote. 'Why? Because this yacht owner claims the miners/electricians are causing such severe damage to the nation that it is essential.' He ended his letter with the contemptuous words, 'Unite us, Heath? Not me.' Patrick Jenkin, a government minister, put his foot in it with what he must have thought was a helpful suggestion. His recommendation that people should 'clean their teeth in the dark' did not meet with approval. He was ridiculed at the time, not least when it was reported that his own house in north London was a blaze of electric light early in the morning, and his gaffe was long remembered, featuring prominently in most newspaper obituaries when he died in 2016.

The effects of the three-day week were immediate. For some, the consequences seemed almost enjoyable, almost a bit of a lark. The spirit of the Blitz was regularly evoked as oil lamps replaced electric lights and candles once more became an essential household item. (A candlemaker in London raised its daily production total to nearly a million because of increased demand. Amongst its more popular lines was a candle in the ample shape of Ted Heath.) For others, the three-day week was a disaster. Earnings went down. Hundreds of thousands of people were put out of work, if only temporarily. Smaller businesses faced cashflow problems and other difficulties. 'Many will not survive if the restrictions last for more than a few weeks,' the director of Aston University's Small Business Centre warned at the end of January. Some businesses proved ingenious in the pursuit of alternative power sources. One Sheffield firm brought a watermill back into use that had last been operational in the middle of the eighteenth century but not many had similar options.

It seemed to some as if Britain was on the slippery slope towards economic ruin. The best option was to get out while they could. During the first two weeks of January, the New Zealand High Commission in London had to deal with three times more inquiries about emigration than usual. Applications to move permanently to Australia and Canada also shot up by as much as a half. Meanwhile, others abroad could scarcely conceal their glee at what was happening. The previous year, the Ugandan dictator, Idi Amin, had offered to do his bit to help Britain out of its economic crisis, suggesting that he would contribute 10,000 Ugandan shillings out of his own savings to any charitable donation to the former colonial masters. Now he rubbed further salt in the wound by reporting that his 'Save Britain Fund' was up and running. On 21 January, he wrote to Heath to say, 'the people of Kigezi district donated one lorry load of vegetables and wheat' and it only needed 'you to send an aircraft to collect this donation urgently before it goes bad.' The offer was politely declined by the British High Commissioner in Uganda but it must have been galling for the government to be mocked by a man they rightly considered little more than a murderous psychopath.

The three-day week restrictions were finally lifted on 7 March 1974. By that date, the crisis had pushed Ted Heath into announcing an election he need not otherwise have held. The miners had gone on strike on 5 February and Heath had called the election two days later. He had lost it (see p. 39) and a new Labour government, led by Harold Wilson, had come to power. The miners' strike had been brought to an end by offering them a 35 per cent pay rise. And the lights had come back on.

Djerba Declaration

Politically and geographically, North Africa would today be very different if an agreement signed on 11 January 1974 had ever been made a reality. Djerba is a large island off the coast of Tunisia and, on that date, it was the venue for a meeting between the seventy-year-old Habib Bourguiba, long the president of that country, and the much younger Muammar Gaddafi, Libya's head of state. The Djerba Declaration, the outcome of that meeting, proposed the unification of the two countries so that a new political entity would emerge – the Arab Islamic Republic – which would have a single constitution, a single president and a single army. Bourguiba would be president of this new state; Gaddafi would be in charge of its armed forces. Referendums would take place in both countries. To describe the signing of the Djerba Declaration as unexpected would be an understatement. There had been little prior discussion of the plan and the agreement that Bourguiba signed was handwritten by Gaddafi at the last minute.

Gaddafi had been calling for Arab unity for some time. In 1971, he had signed an agreement with the leaders of Syria and Egypt to work towards a merger of their three countries in a unified Arab state but arguments over the specific terms of such a merger had soon wrecked the idea. The following year, in December, he had made a speech in Tunis in which he had called for a union between Libya and Tunisia. Although Bourguiba had himself expressed a desire for a 'United States of North Africa' in the past, he had been highly dismissive of Gaddafi's speech, responding with one of his own in which he denied that there had ever been much Arab unity in the past and suggested that Libya was scarcely a united country itself. What had happened to change Bourguiba's mind in the thirteen months leading up to the Djerba Declaration and reconsider the idea is not clear. One historian of North Africa has called the sudden agreement to a union with Libya 'one of the most perplexing moments in Tunisia's political history'. Whatever motivated Bourguiba to put his name to the Declaration (advancing senility which allowed him to be manipulated, according to his enemies; a Machiavellian plan to wean Gaddafi away from prospective alliances with rival countries like Egypt, according to his supporters) his commitment to it turned out to be short-lived. The proposed referendum in Tunisia was postponed indefinitely, the minister in Bourguiba's government most enthusiastic about unity was sacked, and the agreement between the two countries collapsed inside a month.

Commonwealth Games Opens in Christchurch

First held in 1930 as the British Empire Games and later known as the British Empire and Commonwealth Games, the quadrennial sporting competition took place for the tenth time in Christchurch, New Zealand at the beginning of 1974. It was only the second time that the word 'Empire' had been dropped entirely from its official name and it was known just as the Commonwealth Games. Prince Philip represented the Queen at the opening ceremony on 24 January, which included 2,500 children dressed in red, white and blue forming a NZ74 symbol in the middle of the stadium, a Maori *haka* and the traditional march past by competing athletes. Thirty-eight nations, from Australia to Zambia, via others such as Botswana, Fiji, Malaysia, and Trinidad and Tobago, took part and there were medals to be won in 121 events.

This was the first major multinational sporting event to be held since the 1972 Munich Olympics, which had been the scene of a terrorist attack on Israeli athletes. Security, which had not even featured in the original budget for the Christchurch games when it had been put together six years earlier, was now central to the planning and far tighter than it had been for earlier Commonwealth Games. The athletes' village, created from the student accommodation of the local University of Canterbury, was temporarily surrounded by fencing and guards patrolled the perimeter, ensuring that only those with official passes could enter. It could have made for an intimidating atmosphere but the organisers came up with a new idea to make competitors welcome. 'Host families' had volunteered to 'adopt' athletes for the duration of the games. Visitors were given an address where they could, if they wanted, escape the intensity of the athletes' village and relax in the company of an ordinary New Zealand family.

The first day of competition in the athletics, 25 January, was marked by a victory for the host nation in the Men's 10,000 metres when New Zealander Dick Tayler beat several more fancied runners, including the great British hope David Bedford, to cross the finishing line at Queen Elizabeth II Park in a time of 27 minutes and 46.4 seconds. Other victors over the next eight days included the Jamaican sprinter Don Quarrie who took the gold medals in both the 100m and the 200m, the Tanzanian runner Filbert Bayi who set a world record in the 1500m, the Australian Raelene Boyle who, in the women's events, matched Quarrie and won both the 100m and the 200m, and Mary Peters who, in the pentathlon, added another Commonwealth gold medal (she had won in Edinburgh in 1970) to the Olympic one she had collected two years earlier.

Swimming was dominated by the Australians who took the majority of the gold medals in the men's and women's events, although Scotland's David Wilkie came first in both the 200m breaststroke and the 200m medley. The South African-born weightlifter Precious McKenzie, representing England, won the third of four successive Commonwealth gold medals. His fourth, at Edmonton in 1978, came at the age of 42, when he was competing for New Zealand, a country which had so impressed him four years earlier that he had moved there. In the cycling events, the team from Uganda pitched up without any bikes, having wrongly assumed that the games organisers would provide them. People in Christchurch came to their rescue and found them some cycles to ride. Sadly, their new bikes did not help them to success. England and Australia divided the seven gold medals on offer between them. Other sports on display included bowls, badminton, boxing, shooting and wrestling. The final medals table was headed by Australia who took 29 golds to England's 28 and Canada's 25. The hosts, New Zealand, won eight further golds to add to Dick Tayler's.

Ian Wooldridge, then one of Britain's best known sports journalists, had predicted a disaster when he had first arrived and seen what he considered the sub-standard facilities for some of the events. However, he was proved wrong. After two weeks of competition, he was happy to agree with those who 'were declaring the Christchurch Games the friendliest, the most efficient and generally the best... in the Commonwealth series'.

Death of Sam Goldwyn

On 31 January, one of the greatest and most colourful film producers in Hollywood history passed away at his home in Los Angeles. Szmuel Gelbfisz was born in Warsaw, probably in 1879, although he later claimed 1882 as his birth year. He left his native city in his teens and, after sojourns in Hamburg and Birmingham, where he anglicised his name to Samuel Goldfish, he arrived in America in January 1899.

By 1913, he was involved in the movie industry, forming a production company with his brother-in-law, Jesse Lasky. Their first release was a western, *The Squaw Man*, directed by Cecil B DeMille. His name now changed once more, Samuel Goldwyn established the Goldwyn Pictures Corporation in 1916. (Although the biggest of all the studios in Hollywood's Golden Age was MGM, Metro Goldwyn Mayer, Goldwyn had no direct connection with it. It was the result of a sequence of company mergers, one involving Goldwyn Pictures, but Goldwyn had left before the merger. However, MGM did retain the roaring lion which had been used as Goldwyn Pictures' mascot. It remains their logo to this day.) From the mid-1920s onwards, Goldwyn worked as an independent producer with great success. Amongst the many films to which his name was attached were *Dead End*, *Wuthering Heights* and *The Little Foxes*. In 1946, *The Best Years of Our Lives*, a Samuel Goldwyn Production, won the Oscar for Best Picture.

He became as famous for his 'Goldwynisms', which were widely quoted both during his life and after his death, as for his movies. Sadly, some of the most memorable of these verbal mishaps and contradictions ('A verbal contract isn't worth the paper it's written on'; 'I read part of it all the way through'; 'Anyone who goes to a psychiatrist ought to have his head examined') are apocryphal. However, it may be the case that he said some of the many mangled remarks attributed to him, even though he himself grew weary of the belief that he couldn't speak English properly. 'Goldwynisms,' he once said to the writer Garson Kanin. 'Don't talk to me about Goldwynisms, for Christ's sake! You want to hear some Goldwynisms, go talk to Jesse Lasky.' As Kanin later wrote, this was 'a pure Goldwynism, created as he was attempting to deny the existence of such a thing'. Whatever the truth about the assorted quotes attached to his name, it would certainly be delightful to believe that, when an underling once pointed out that Goldwyn couldn't make a film version of Radclyffe Hall's then controversial novel, *The Well of Loneliness*, because the central characters were lesbian, the mogul replied, 'That's OK, we'll make them Albanians.'

February

A fire in a multi-storey building in Sao Paulo causes the deaths of 179 people. In Britain, the first of two general elections in the year takes Labour's Harold Wilson back to Number 10 Downing Street as prime minister after four years of Tory government. A bomb tears apart a coach travelling along the M62 motorway in Yorkshire, killing a dozen people and injuring many more. Skylab 4 returns to Earth, bringing back three astronauts from the American space station. A Vermeer painting is stolen in Hampstead. Grenada wins its independence. The dissident writer Aleksandr Solzhenitsyn is expelled from the Soviet Union. Alison Steadman and Myra Frances share the first lesbian kiss on British TV.

Joelma Building Fire

The Joelma Building was the name given to a 25-storey skyscraper in the centre of Sao Paulo, Brazil which was the main office block for the banking company Banco Crefisul S/A. At around 8.50am on 1 February 1974, it became the scene of one of the worst fires in a high-rise building before the attack on the World Trade Center in New York in 2001. On the twelfth floor an air conditioning unit short-circuited, overheated and then burst into flames. Because so much flammable material had been used in the interior furnishings of the Joelma, and because there were no sprinkler systems in place, it took only twenty minutes for the fire to spread to many of the other floors. Stairwells filled with smoke, preventing people trying to escape from using them. A lack of emergency exits and lights added to their confusion and terror.

A young woman named Clara Gomes had been among the first to smell the smoke and raise the alarm. Once she made it down to street level she was appalled to see the speed with which the fire had seized hold of the Joelma. 'When I got there,' she told a journalist, 'the flames were already racing up through the building.' Fire crews were alerted but held up en route, 'inching their way through the traffic jams that were now rapidly building up in the city centre', as one report put it. When they arrived at the Joelma, they were able to lead many workers in the building to safety but the heat and smoke in the stairwells prevented would-be rescuers from reaching the building's higher floors. Not only that but the ladders they had could only reach just over halfway up the building. It was very soon impossible to get beyond the 11th storey. Dozens of people on the floors above, cut off by the fire, took to the roof and there were initially hopes that they could be rescued by helicopter. These were dashed when it was realised that the intense heat and the billowing plumes of smoke had made any landing there impossible. Desperation had taken hold of many of those trapped. According to Clara Gomes, 'Already people were jumping from the windows'. At least 40 anguished individuals, losing hope, took this option but none of them survived.

With firefighters on the scene, pumping thousands of gallons of water at it, the fire began to die down between 10.30 and 11am. By mid-afternoon, with no more material to feed it, it had simply burnt itself out. However, by that time, at least 179 people who had worked in the Joelma Building had died and another 300 had suffered burns and injuries caused by smoke inhalation. Thirteen victims were found in the shell of one of the building's elevators, so badly burned that they were never properly identified. The death toll at the Joelma was so high that it led to a re-examination and tightening of fire safety regulations not only in Brazil itself but in countries around the world. The building itself remained closed for four years while substantial reconstruction work was undertaken. When it opened again, it was renamed *Edificio Praça da Bandeira* ('Flag Square Building') after the plaza facing it. The name 'Joelma' was too tainted by the horrors of the day of the fire.

Election in Britain

At the beginning of 1974, the British prime minister was Ted Heath. He had come to power with the Tory victory in the 1970 election after five years as leader of the opposition. His premiership had had its successes (he had fulfilled his long-standing aim of taking Britain into the EEC) but it had faced crisis after crisis. Five states of emergency had been declared in less than four years. On 7 February, confronted by a multitude of problems, from increasing troubles in Northern Ireland and industrial turmoil throughout the UK to unrest and rebellion on his own backbenches, Heath made what has been described as 'one of the great miscalculations of British political history'. He called a general election. He had no need to do so until the following year but he was determined to gain a new mandate for his government and his policies. 'Do you want a strong government which has clear authority for the future to take the decisions which will be needed?' he asked in his TV announcement of the election. Most people probably did but the question of whether they thought that government should be led by Ted Heath was still to be answered. What followed was, in the words of the historian Dominic Sandbrook, 'one of the most tumultuous election campaigns in modern history'.

Tory chances of success were not helped by Heath's awkward and often difficult personality. The prime minister could all too easily appear rude, arrogant and out of touch. 'Instead of trying to speak to people,' the future Foreign Secretary, Douglas Hurd, then one of his political aides, later wrote, 'Mr Heath would too often speak at them'. As the historian Andy Beckett puts it in his account of Britain in the 1970s, 'For a politician with a liking for consensus he had a striking ability to enrage'. Heath's opponent was Harold Wilson, a wily political operator who had been prime minister between 1964 and 1970, and had twice won closely fought elections in the previous decade. He was not the force he had once been but he was still a formidable campaigner. However, political disillusionment with both parties was on the increase. Many voters would have agreed with the assertion in the *Sun* newspaper, previously a staunch Labour supporter: 'We're Sick of the Ted and Harold Show'.

On the very first day of the campaign Heath announced a significant relaxation of the three-day week (see p. 26), one which would be immediately noticeable to most voters. The TV channels would be allowed to broadcast after 10.30pm. Despite all the problems the Tory government had faced, the polls initially suggested that victory would be theirs. Even top Labour politicians were gloomy about the party's prospects. Six days before the vote, Tony Benn accompanied Wilson to a rally and then noted in his diary, 'I think he does realise that he is perhaps within a week of the end of his political career'. On election day itself, after an unusually brief campaigning period of only three weeks, the nation turned out to vote on Thursday 28 February. The Tories were still optimistic. Reporting a last-minute poll that gave the Conservatives a significant lead, the *Daily Mail* ran a headline reading, 'A Handsome Win for Heath'. It was not to be.

Concerns that the electorate was disenchanted with all politicians and all too likely to stay at home proved misplaced. The percentage of voters who turned out to exercise their democratic right was high, but the outcome of the election was frustrating for all parties. The great strength of the first-past-the-post system is supposed to be that it produces a decisive result. In February 1974, it most certainly did not. Labour emerged as the largest party with 301 seats, but this was still 17 short of giving it an overall majority. Despite polling marginally more votes, the Tories had won only 297 seats. The Liberals had increased their number of seats from 6 to 14. One statistic that seems almost incredible today is that only 23 female MPs were elected in February 1974, three fewer than had made it into the House of Commons at the previous general election in 1970.

Ted Heath was at first unwilling to leave office, hoping that he would be able to come to some kind of agreement with the Liberals, led by Jeremy Thorpe, which would enable him to remain as prime minister. Thorpe, tempted by the prospect of high office in any coalition government, was interested. His party, however, demanded promises of electoral reform. In return for cooperation with the Tories, members wanted proportional representation so that the number of Liberal MPs in Westminster would in future more closely reflect the number of votes cast for the party in national elections. Heath was not prepared to countenance this, offering only the possibility of an official enquiry into electoral reform, because he knew that anything more would alienate his own MPs. He was also wary of Thorpe's wish to become Home Secretary in any coalition government. 'I had been warned by the Secretary of the Cabinet,' he wrote later in his autobiography, 'that there were matters in Thorpe's private life, as yet undisclosed to the public, which might make this a highly unsuitable position for him to hold.' The discussions between Tories and Liberals came to nothing. (Thorpe's career did indeed end in scandal a few years later when he was tried at the Old Bailey on charges of conspiring to murder a former male lover. He was acquitted but his political life was effectively over.) Attempts to woo the Ulster Unionists into some kind of formal pact also failed. The PM had now to face the fact that his resignation was inevitable. Early on the morning of 4 March, a Monday, Heath held his last meeting with senior figures from his cabinet. 'It was not a cheerful occasion,' one reported with typically British understatement.

That evening, Harold Wilson returned to Downing Street as prime minister. People who were gathered outside either cheered or booed, according to their political sympathies, when he stepped out of his official car. Wilson did not look wholly delighted by the prospect ahead of him. In the words of Andy Beckett, he 'walked slowly – almost trudged – the few yards to the front door of No. 10, with his shoulders slack and his back to the crowd. On the doorstep he turned and waved, a little woodenly, without any apparent joy. He gave the briefest flicker of a smile.' A journalist called out to ask him what it felt like to be back. Wilson paused for quite some time, glancing twice at his wife before replying. 'We've got a job to do,' he announced. 'We can only do that job as one people, and I'm going right in to start that job now.'

M62 Coach Bombing

Late on the evening of 3 February a coach departed Manchester. Specially commissioned to carry British soldiers back to their bases from weekend leave, it was travelling along the M62 motorway at about 60mph, en route to Catterick in North Yorkshire, when a 25-pound bomb that had been hidden in the luggage lockers exploded. The entire back portion of the coach was destroyed but somehow the driver, Rowland Handley, succeeded in steering his mangled vehicle to the side of the road. Bleeding heavily from injuries caused by flying debris, he staggered out of his seat to investigate the wreckage. It was an appalling scene. He saw 'a young child of two or three lying in the road. It was dead. There were bodies all over.' Within moments of the explosion, other motorists were stopping to see what help they could offer. 'The smell was what upset me really,' one of them later said. 'It was dark so you couldn't see how bad the injuries really were, but it was the smell of it. It was absolutely total carnage.'

The entrance hall of the westbound section of Hartshead Moor service station near Brighouse became an improvised first aid station where the wounded could be treated before transfer to nearby hospitals. Eleven people were killed as a result of the M62 bombing and fifty others were injured, some severely. (One died of his injuries a few days later.) An entire family – Corporal Clifford Haughton, his wife Linda and their two sons, five-year-old Lee and two-year-old Robert – were amongst the dead. They had been in seats directly above the bomb.

Ten days after the bombing, a young Englishwoman named Judith Ward was arrested in Liverpool where she had been sleeping rough and hoping to find money and opportunity to travel to Ireland. In police custody, she eventually claimed responsibility for placing the bomb in the coach and forensic scientists found faint traces of nitroglycerin both on her fingernails and on personal possessions, including her duffel bag. Despite numerous inconsistencies in the various statements, 28 in all, which Ward gave to the police and despite a dozen witnesses willing to state that she was in the Cotswolds just before the day of the bombing, working as a groom for Chipperfield's Circus, she was sent for trial. In October, she appeared at Wakefield Crown Court, charged with 15 offences, including 12 counts of murder. She pleaded not guilty. The prosecution relied on Ward's own confessions, which she had retracted, and on the scientific evidence that she had been in contact with explosives; the defence argued that she was 'a female Walter Mitty', that her confessions were all rambling fantasies, and that the forensic evidence was nowhere near as strong as the prosecution was claiming.

On 4 November, Ward was found guilty on all charges and sentenced to life imprisonment.

Following her conviction, the Provisional IRA issued a statement in which they announced unambiguously that she had never been a member of the organisation and that she had nothing whatsoever to do with the bombing. It was too late to do her any good. Ward's conviction was the first in a series of miscarriages of justice in cases involving Provisional IRA bomb atrocities. She served nearly 18 years in prison before it was finally overturned and she was released in May 1992. The identity of the real M62 bomber remains uncertain and nobody else has ever been arrested and convicted of the crime.

Grenada Wins Independence

By 1974 Britain had been slowly losing its empire for decades. India had gained its independence in 1948. Independent African nations had emerged, from Ghana to Kenya, in the 1950s and 1960s. The latter decade had also seen Jamaica, Trinidad and Tobago, and Barbados cut direct ties with London. In the 1970s, it was time for Britain's smaller possessions in the Caribbean to assert their freedom. The first to do so was Grenada. The island's original colonial masters had been French but it had been ceded to the British in 1763 after the Seven Years' War. For more than two centuries it remained part of the empire.

The movement towards self-government, first mooted in the early decades of the twentieth century, began to gather strength in the years after the Second World War. In 1958, Grenada was one of a number of Caribbean islands to come together in the West Indies Federation, a short-lived political union that never really established a way of working and collapsed after only four years. In 1967, it was declared one of the West Indies Associated States which meant that the island had control over its domestic affairs but the British government still remained in charge of defence and foreign policy.

On 7 February 1974, full independence finally arrived for Grenada and Eric Gairy became prime minister of the new nation. Gairy had been a major force in Grenadian politics for decades. Originally a trade unionist, he had founded the Grenada United Labour Party in 1950, when he was a young man in his late twenties, and had spent two periods in power in the 1960s before independence, firstly as chief minister and then as premier. He was not, however, by any means universally popular with Grenadians. After independence, he grew increasingly dictatorial. A militia, the Special Reserve Police, informally known as the Mongoose Gang, was under his control and acted effectively as his private army, threatening and even, it is alleged, killing his political opponents.

One of Gairy's more unusual interests was in the subject of UFOs. He was convinced that they were alien visitors and that, in his own words, 'persons from outer space are studying us, or perhaps living among us as earthlings'. He even went so far as to address a committee of the UN and suggest that the organisation would be shirking its global responsibilities if it didn't take 'a serious look at the UFO phenomenon'. The UN did not share Gairy's concerns about possible aliens amongst us and he soon had more pressing matters to consider. As his regime grew more oppressive, his political rivals within Grenada plotted against him. During another visit by Gairy to the UN in 1979, amidst rumours that the Mongoose Gang were planning to assassinate opposition leaders while he was out of the country, there was an armed coup and he was overthrown.

Skylab 4 Returns

Skylab was the first American space station, launched into orbit around the Earth in May 1973. Three crews of astronauts spent time there. Slightly confusingly, the previous manned missions had been on Skylab 2 and Skylab 3. Skylab 4, despite the numbering, was only the third one to be crewed. (Skylab 1 refers to the launch of the station.) The rocket which propelled Gerald Carr, Edward Gibson and William Pogue into space blasted off on 16 November 1973. For all of them it was their first spaceflight (and, as it turned out, their only one) and together they spent the then record period of 84 days in space.

On arrival at the station, they were surprised to find three figures in flight suits already in residence. These turned out to be dummies left behind as a joke by their Skylab 3 predecessors. The astronauts were also taken aback by how large their new home was. It was even possible to get lost in it. Ed Gibson later described how his two colleagues went looking for him at one point and missed him because he was crouched down in an area known as the Orbital Workshop. 'When I finally floated into view, they said, "Where the heck have you been?"' Every third day they could speak to their families for ten to fifteen minutes. It was an important link for the men, although some family members seemed a little blasé about the conversations across the vast distances of space. On one such occasion, Ed Gibson was launched upon what he thought was an eloquent description of the wonders he could see from Skylab when he heard his youngest daughter say, 'Mummy, can I go out and play?'

The successes of the previous two missions, Skylabs 2 and 3, placed extra pressure on the three men of Skylab 4. Mission Control had gained an unrealistic idea of the amount of work they could get out of Carr and his colleagues, and their schedule was punishingly hard. One of the men, William Pogue, had suffered a bout of space sickness soon after arriving at the station and all of them found it difficult to maintain what Ed Gibson later described as 'nothing but a 33-day fire drill' in which their time was micromanaged down to the minute by the NASA staff in Houston. Tensions grew between the three men in space and Mission Control. 'We swallowed a lot of problems for a lot of days,' Carr later admitted, 'because we were reluctant to admit publicly that we were not getting things done right.' After some weeks he made the decision to try to explain the difficulties he and his small team were having and this airing of concerns made life easier for all. Because of the problems that definitely existed in those first weeks, rumours persist that the three astronauts effectively went on strike at one point during the mission. The more mundane truth is that there was a communications failure and they were out of contact with Houston for a time. 'There was no "strike in space" by any stretch of the imagination,' Gerald Carr later wrote. 'What could we threaten to do, go live on the moon?'

The second six weeks of the crew's stay aboard the station proved far more satisfying for them than the first six weeks. They had been initially scheduled to return home early in January after something approaching 60 days but the plan had always been that extensions to the time could be made on a weekly basis if all was going well.

This was certainly the case. The men themselves were now in cheerful spirits and still physically fit. The station itself was in good shape. The weekly extensions of their stay occurred throughout January. Eventually, five days after completing a fourth and final spacewalk outside Skylab 4, the three astronauts completed their record-setting mission. It was time for them to head home. The command module splashed down in the Pacific on 8 February and they were picked up by USS *New Orleans*. Skylab itself finally returned to Earth in July 1979, breaking up as it entered the atmosphere and scattering debris over parts of the Indian Ocean and of Western Australia.

Vermeer Stolen

The Guitar Player is a painting by Johannes Vermeer, one of only a handful of his works in the UK, which is to be found at Kenwood House in Hampstead. It was from there that it was stolen on the night of 23 February 1974. Somebody using a sledgehammer smashed through a steel-barred window on the ground floor, grabbed the painting off the wall and escaped before the alarm could be raised. So famous a work of art would be difficult to dispose of. 'We are looking for either a master thief or a madman,' a spokesman for Scotland Yard opined. 'It could be the work of someone who does not know what he has done or has no idea of the value of what he has got. But so far we think it is a master thief who has planned the operation over a number of years.' According to Robert Volpe, an American private detective who specialised in tracking down stolen art works, this putative master thief must have known the person to whom he was going to sell the painting. How else could he make a profit from his crime? 'What's this guy going to do,' Volpe said at the time, 'go up to a dealer and say "Hey, I'm looking to sell my Vermeer?"'

The police suspected that the painting might have been stolen expressly so that a ransom could be demanded for its return and, indeed, anonymous ransom messages soon began to be received. One stipulated that two IRA prisoners serving life sentences should be transferred from a British to an Irish jail. Another, made by phone, sought a ransom in the form of a million dollars' worth of food to be distributed to the poor in the newly independent West Indian nation of Grenada. At one point, a small piece of the canvas was sent in an envelope to the *Times* together with a typewritten note bemoaning the fact that 'capitalist society values its treasures more than humanity' and threatening to burn the painting.

For just over two months it seemed as if the Vermeer might have disappeared forever. The frame had been discovered soon after the theft, damaged at one corner, but of the painting itself there was no sign. All attempts to track it down failed, including calling in the help of a psychic who claimed to have 'seen' its whereabouts while doing her ironing. After another anonymous tip-off, Scotland Yard officers finally found *The Guitar Player* on 7 May. The painting was in the churchyard of St Bartholomew-the-Great where, in the words of a police spokesman, it was 'propped up against a gravestone, wrapped in newspaper and tied with a string'. Apart from small signs of dampness, it was undamaged. It was returned to Kenwood House where it can still be seen today. The thief has never been identified. Some have thought that it was Rose Dugdale, an upper-class, Oxford-educated supporter of the IRA who took part in April 1974 in a raid on Russborough House, County Wicklow in which 19 Old Master paintings were stolen. She was arrested, tried and served a prison sentence for that crime but has never been charged with stealing *The Guitar Player*. The journalist Simon Jenkins has speculated that the person who took the Vermeer from Kenwood House was someone who was simply obsessed with the woman depicted in it and then 'found her too hot to handle'.

Solzhenitsyn Expelled from Soviet Union

According to Harrison Salisbury, one-time Moscow correspondent of the *New York Times*, Aleksandr Solzhenitsyn was 'a literary genius whose talent matches that of Dostoevsky, Turgenev, Tolstoy, Gorky'. In the 1960s the Russian poet Yevgeny Yevtushenko called him 'our only living classic'. There have been few dissenters from this idea of his greatness, although Gore Vidal, ever the controversialist, once described him as 'a bad novelist and a fool', remarking that this was a combination that 'usually makes for great popularity in the US'. Solzhenitsyn's fame may have faded a little in the years since his death in 2008 but he remains a key figure in twentieth-century Russian literature.

At times this must have seemed unlikely, not least to the writer himself. Solzhenitsyn, who had spent years in labour camps after the Second World War, mostly in what is now Kazakhstan, found himself at odds with the Soviet regime throughout most of his literary career. 'During all the years until 1961,' he later wrote, 'not only was I convinced I should never see a single line of mine in print in my lifetime, but, also, I scarcely dared allow any of my close acquaintances to read anything I had written because I feared this would become known.'

His brief time in favour with the authorities came in the early 1960s when his novella *One Day in the Life of Ivan Denisovich*, based on his experiences in the camps, was published, with the express permission of the Soviet leader, Nikita Khrushchev. Eager to disassociate himself from the horrors of Stalinism, Khrushchev had presided over a period of comparative liberalisation. Subjects which had previously been taboo in the arts, such as the conditions in the Gulag, could now be acknowledged.

Solzhenitsyn's new artistic freedom did not last long. With Khrushchev ousted from power in 1964 and a more repressive cultural policy re-established, he found it impossible once more to have his work published. Attempts to expose the full horrors of the forced labour camps in his three-volume *magnum opus*, *The Gulag Archipelago*, were actively suppressed. He was expelled from the official Writers' Union in 1969. In the West, however, his reputation and status as a dissident only grew. He was awarded the 1970 Nobel Prize for Literature for 'the ethical force with which he has pursued the indispensable traditions of Russian literature'. Fearful that he would not be allowed back into the Soviet Union if he travelled to Stockholm for the ceremony, he was unable to accept the prize in person. A suggestion that he might receive it in the Swedish Embassy in Moscow was also vetoed, this time because the Swedes were wary of offending the USSR.

The more he was lauded in the West, the more Solzhenitsyn became anathema to the authorities in his own country. By the beginning of 1974, it was almost impossible for him to function as a writer in the Soviet Union or even as a citizen. Ordered to put in an appearance at the Moscow Public Prosecutor's office, he refused and instead alerted Western media, including the BBC, to what was happening. On 12 February, eight men burst into his flat and he was arrested on a charge of treason. 'So that's your game!' he is reported to have shouted at them. Fearing the worst, he spent the night in a cell with two other men. The following day, he was expelled from the country and stripped of his Soviet citizenship. He was driven to the airport and put on a flight to Frankfurt, West Germany. Solzhenitsyn had only ever left the Soviet Union once before, as a Red Army soldier, advancing into Germany at the end of the Second World War, and he had never been on a plane. On landing in Frankfurt, a KGB officer thrust some Deutschmarks into his hand and abandoned him into the care of a welcoming committee of West German officials. He was initially given shelter by fellow writer Heinrich Böll at his house in the little village of Langenbroich in North Rhine Westphalia. The following month he moved to Zurich where his family joined him.

In December 1974, he was finally able to attend the Nobel Banquet in Stockholm and give the speech he had been unable to give four years earlier. 'The Swedish

Academy and the Nobel Foundation have probably never had as much bother with anyone as they have had with me,' he began and went on to offer his listeners an eloquent defence of freedom of speech and the importance of a nation facing up to the truth about itself. 'Woe to that nation,' he said, 'whose literature is cut short by the intrusion of force. This is not merely interference with freedom of the press but the sealing up of a nation's heart, the excision of its memory.'

First Lesbian Kiss on British TV

It's sometimes assumed that the first lesbian kiss on British TV was on *Brookside* in 1994 when Anna Friel, playing Beth Jordache, engaged Margaret Clemence (Nicola Stephenson) in a passionate embrace. In truth, the taboo had been broken nearly twenty years earlier in a short play called 'Girl', one of a series of single dramas made at the Pebble Mill studios in Birmingham entitled *Second City Firsts*. First broadcast by BBC 2 on 25 February and written by James Robson, 'Girl' was the story, seen retrospectively, of the love affair between two WRAC soldiers, one of whom is about to leave the service and encounters her former lover. The central characters, and pioneer kissers, were played by Alison Steadman and Myra Frances.

Steadman was then at the beginning of a career which has seen her become one of the country's best-known actresses, familiar to audiences from her frequent roles in the films of Mike Leigh, her former husband, and in a host of TV series from *The Singing Detective* to *Gavin & Stacey*.

'When I was offered the part I felt quite nervous,' she later said but she went on to praise the approach of the drama's director, Peter Gill. 'He was great because he didn't fuss about the fact they were two women or that they had to kiss. He said it was just a love story.' The producer proved rather more worried about the scene than Gill because he came to watch rehearsals in order to monitor what was happening and a special announcement, warning anybody likely to be offended of what they were about to see, was broadcast just before the play aired. When it went out, Steadman's greatest concern was that her parents, who lived in a quiet suburban area of Liverpool, might be embarrassed by the scene and any furore it caused but 'my mum said she thought it was great and was very moved by it'.

Steadman and Frances's onscreen kiss actually preceded by five years the first gay kiss between two men on British TV which arrived in 1979 in a 'Play for Today' with the appropriate title of Coming Out. The pioneering 'Girl' was not broadcast again until 2016 when it was included in a collection of groundbreaking LGBT programmes on BBC Store, a short-lived video-on-demand service.

March

The German car manufacturer Volkswagen launches a
new model which they hope will be an equally successful
replacement for their legendary Beetle. Agatha Christie's
play The Mousetrap, already a long-running triumph,
opens in a different theatre. A Second World War
Japanese soldier finally surrenders nearly thirty years after
the war's end. In London an attempt is made to kidnap
Princess Anne. In China peasant farmers make an
astonishing discovery while digging a well.

Volkswagen Golf

The very first Volkswagen Golf rolled off the assembly line in Wolfsburg, Germany in March 1974. In the next nine years more than 6 million others followed it. The Golf Mark 1 was designed to be the successor to the company's enormously successful Beetle which had been around since the 1930s and was still being produced in the first years of the twenty-first century. Its designer was not a German but an Italian – Giorgetto Giugiaro, a man who was voted Car Designer of the Century in a 1999 poll of automotive journalists. Over the course of a glittering career, Giugiaro produced designs for an array of major car brands, from Alfa Romeo and BMW to Lotus and SEAT. The ill-fated DMC DeLorean, now most famous for its appearance in the *Back to the Future* films, was Giugiaro's work. He did not restrict himself to automobiles. He was also responsible for designing watches for Seiko, cameras for Nikon, an organ for Lausanne Cathedral, and a seafront promenade at the Tuscan town of Porto San Stefano. One of his few undoubted failures was his design for a new pasta shape, 'Marille', which never quite caught on with lovers of Italian food.

An important choice for Volkswagen was what to call the Beetle's replacement. During the development stage a number of possibilities including 'Blizzard' and 'Caribe' were suggested, only to be rejected. What was needed was a simple, memorable name that could be clearly understood across international boundaries and in a variety of languages. 'Golf' was eventually chosen, not only referring to the game but also to the German word *Golfstrom*, meaning 'Gulf stream'.

At the time of its first appearance, Volkswagen described their new car in strictly utilitarian terms: 'The Golf offers a maximum in usable space and safety. It is uncompromisingly geared towards practical use. The low waistline allows for good all-round visibility, the sloping front hood provides a view of the road right up to the car. Thanks to the drawn-down rear window, reversing is no problem.' However, in retrospect, with the passing of the decades, it has seemed a more momentous occasion in the company's history. According to Klaus Bischoff, the man who was Volkswagen's Chief Designer between 2007 and 2022, 'The step from the Beetle to the Golf was revolutionary... a completely new vehicle layout was created at the time'. The main design elements of the Golf 1 are still to be found in every Golf today.

The Mousetrap Transfers to the St Martin's Theatre

Famously, Agatha Christie's *The Mousetrap* is the longest-running play in theatrical history. Since its London opening night on 25 November 1952, after earlier performances the previous month in Nottingham, Manchester, Birmingham and other cities, it has clocked up tens of thousands of performances. The original 1952 cast included film star and future director Richard Attenborough together with his wife Sheila Sim but the initial notices were not entirely complimentary. According to one reviewer in the *Daily Herald*, Attenborough was 'lacking presence' and the climax 'left us more dazed than excited... I felt faintly cheated'. A more generous writer in the *Bradford Observer*, after seeing one of the out-of-London previews, proved correct, however, in his prediction that 'this play should run for a long time in the metropolis'. Although, the fact that it is still pulling in the crowds more than seventy years later would probably have surprised him.

Since plays tended to have shorter runs in the past, *The Mousetrap* had already become the longest-running show in British theatre history by the spring of 1958 and, at that point, in the words of producer Stephen Waley-Cohen, 'it began to develop its own momentum'. Seeing it soon became, like visiting Madame Tussauds or watching the Changing of the Guard, an essential component of a tourist trip to London. On Saturday 23 March 1974, the play finished its 21-year run at its original home, the Ambassadors Theatre. On the following Monday, it opened in the nearby (and larger) St Martin's Theatre where it has been performed ever since. In all those decades there has been only one hiatus. During the pandemic, the St Martin's, like all other theatres, was obliged to close its doors but it was one of the first to re-open when restrictions were lifted.

The Mousetrap had an unusual genesis. It began life as a 30-minute radio drama broadcast by the BBC on 30 May 1947 as part of an evening of programmes to celebrate Queen Mary's 80th birthday. In the same year, this was turned into a TV version. In 1948, Christie used the radio play as the basis for a short story entitled 'Three Blind Mice' which was published in the American magazine *Cosmopolitan* and later in a US collection of her short stories. (Although the story was published in a British magazine soon after it was written, it has never since appeared in this country.) The writer saw further potential in the plot and wrote the stage play. Because there had recently been another West End show called 'Three Blind Mice', she sought another title and *The Mousetrap*, a reference to the play-within-a-play in *Hamlet*, was chosen.

Not everyone has been happy with the play's longevity. 'The St Martin's Theatre is one of the most attractive playhouses in the West End,' wrote the theatre critic Charles Spencer in 2011, 'and it is tragic that it has been filled with such tedious tosh for so long.' What *is* the lasting appeal of *The Mousetrap*? Agatha Christie herself suggested an answer to this. 'It is the sort of play you can take anyone to,' she once said. 'It is not really frightening. It is not really horrible. It is not really a farce, but it has a little bit of all these things, and perhaps that satisfies a lot of different people.' On its return to St Martin's, after the enforced break of the lockdown, one newspaper writer, hailing it as 'the cleverest murder mystery of the British theatre', predicted, tongue-in-cheek, that it 'could run forever'. Fifty years after it swapped theatres, and more than seventy after its premiere, it often seems as if he could be right.

Hiroo Onoda Surrenders

After the Imperial Japanese Army surrendered in August 1945, bringing to an end the war in the Pacific, a significant number of Japanese soldiers fought on. Mostly isolated on small islands, they had either not received word that the game was up, had refused to believe the news or had decided that their honour demanded they continue to bear arms. One of the very last of these holdouts, who did not surrender until March 1974, more than 28 years after the majority of his compatriots had laid down their weapons, was Hiroo Onoda.

Born in Kainan, a small city on Honshu, Japan, in March 1922, Onoda worked as a teenager for a trading company in China before enlisting in the army in 1940. Four years later, and now an intelligence officer, he was sent to the island of Lubang in the Philippines. His instructions were to join forces with other soldiers already stationed there and do everything he could to withstand the increasing US attacks on Lubang. He was explicitly told not to surrender in any circumstances. When US troops landed on the island in 1945 and took control of it, Onoda retreated to the hills with three comrades. They embarked on a guerrilla campaign which was to last long after the Japanese surrender in September. In October 1945, Onoda saw a leaflet which had been dropped from the air with news of the end of the war but he assumed it was a trick and ignored it. He and his fellow holdouts decided to fight on, hiding in the remotest parts of the island and occasionally exchanging fire with local police. In the autumn of 1949, one of the four men walked away from the group and surrendered several months later. Another was killed in a skirmish with a search party in 1954. Onoda and his last companion, Private Kinshichi Kozuka, continued their lonely guerrilla fight for 18 more years until Kozuka was killed by police in October 1972. Onoda was now on his own. He might have stayed in the jungle until his own death had it not been for a man named Norio Suzuki.

Born in 1949, four years after Onoda had first taken to the hills, Suzuki was an adventurous young man, with an urge to make a name for himself. When news came that a wartime holdout was still operating on Lubang, he saw his opportunity. In his own words, he wanted to track down, 'Lieutenant Onoda, a panda, and the Abominable Snowman, in that order'. He travelled to the Philippine island and began his search for his first quarry. Perhaps surprisingly, Suzuki was soon successful. He encountered Onoda for the first time in early 1974. Onoda's first instinct was to shoot what he later called 'this hippie boy' but Suzuki saved his own life by calling out, 'Onoda-san, the emperor and the people of Japan are worried about you.' Still wary, the holdout soldier engaged his unexpected visitor in conversation but he refused to surrender until he received a direct order from his superior officer. His former commanding officer, Major Yoshimi Taniguchi, was now an old man who worked in a bookshop back in Japan but he agreed to accompany Suzuki to Lubang.

On 9 March, Taniguchi met Onoda and gave him the order for which the soldier had been waiting. He had done his duty, he was told. Honour was satisfied. Nearly thirty years later than most of his compatriots, he could surrender. Onoda handed over his sword, his rifle, ammunition and a number of hand grenades. He also delivered up the dagger which his mother had presented to him before he left for Lubang so that he had the means to kill himself if honour demanded it. Onoda arrived back in Japan to find himself, if not a hero, then very definitely a celebrity.

While Onoda attempted to cope with the bewildering change from solitary jungle guerrilla to star of the Japanese media, Suzuki went in search of the other two creatures on his must-find list. A panda was not too difficult to locate but a Yeti proved more of a challenge, although he claimed to have seen one in the distance in 1975. Eleven years later he returned to the Himalayas to renew his quest but died in an avalanche in November 1986, still hopeful that he might one day capture an Abominable Snowman.

Onoda rapidly grew weary of the attention he received in Japan and found it difficult to adjust to a country so different to the one he had left as a young soldier. Little more than a year after departing the jungle, he emigrated to Brazil where he became a cattle rancher and a prominent member of the Japanese community in the small town of Terenos in the state of Matto Grosso do Sul. He stayed there for nearly a decade before returning to his homeland in 1984 and establishing the 'Onoda Nature School', an educational camp for disadvantaged youngsters. Hiroo Onoda died in a Tokyo hospital on 16 January 2014. He was 91 years old.

Onoda was not the last of the holdouts. That ambivalent honour goes to Teruo Nakamura who was found on the small Indonesian island of Morotai in December 1974. Nakamura was from Taiwan. He had joined a group of Taiwanese volunteers to the Japanese forces in 1943 and could not even speak Japanese so his discovery did not gain the vast media coverage that Onoda's did. In the decades after Nakamura's surrender, there were persistent rumours that other holdout soldiers still lurked in the jungle fastnesses of remote islands but none was ever found.

Attempt to Kidnap Princess Anne

At around 8pm on Wednesday 20 March, Princess Anne and her husband of a few months, Captain Mark Phillips, were on their way home after a charity film screening. As their limousine headed down The Mall in the direction of Buckingham Palace, a white Ford Escort was being driven erratically in front of it. Eventually, it forced Princess Anne's chauffeur to stop. The driver of the Escort, later identified as one Ian Ball, jumped out of the car, waving two handguns. Inspector James Beaton, Anne's personal police protection officer, who had been sitting in the limousine's passenger seat, swiftly exited the limousine to confront the man. Ball shot him in the shoulder. Despite his wound, Beaton attempted to return fire but his aim was unsurprisingly poor and his gun, after firing once, jammed. Ball moved to the rear door of the limousine and began to tug at its handle. As he did so, the princess and her husband were struggling to keep the door shut. Beaton had succeeded in getting back into the car through the opposite rear door and he now tried to shield the princess, receiving another two wounds for his troubles. The chauffeur, Alexander Callender, who also tried to intervene, was shot in the chest. In all the melee, Ball finally managed to pull open the door on his side and seized Princess Anne by the arm, shouting, 'Please come out, you've got to come.' 'Not bloody likely,' she replied. An undignified and dangerous tussle took place during which part of the princess's dress was ripped. It was at this point, she told Michael Parkinson on his TV chatshow in 1980, that she became angry. Until then, she said, 'I was scrupulously polite because I thought it was silly to be too rude.' Since her would-be kidnapper was waving a gun and had already shot two people, she was probably right. 'The back of my dress split,' she went on, 'and that was his most dangerous moment. I lost my rag at that stage.'

While Anne was losing her rag, other people, both police officers and passers-by, arrived at the scene and tried to intervene. PC Michael Hills, who had been on patrol nearby, approached Ball and was shot in the stomach. He fell to the ground but was able to radio for help. A journalist named Brian McConnell became the fourth man to be wounded when he approached the gunman with the words, 'Don't be silly, old boy. Put the gun down'. Instead of doing that, Ball shot him in the chest. As the would-be kidnapper then turned back to the royal limo, Ronald Russell, a former boxer who had seen PC Hills fall to the ground and left his own car to find out what was happening, punched him hard in the back of the head. Much now happened in a brief period of time. The princess backed out of the car on the opposite side to Ball who reacted by trying to go round the limo and seize her. Russell punched him again, this time in the face. Anne jumped back in the car, slamming shut the door. By now, more police officers summoned by PC Hills's radio call were at the scene. Ian Ball began to realise that his plan was not working as smoothly as he had anticipated. He decided it was time to leave and took off, running through St James's Park, pursued by Detective Constable Peter Edmonds, one of the newly arrived officers. Throwing his coat over the fugitive's head, Edmonds rugby-tackled him to the ground. Support for Edmonds arrived and Ian Ball was placed under arrest.

It soon became apparent that he had been preparing for the kidnap for some time. He had adopted the pseudonym of John Williams and done his best to eradicate his identity as Ian Ball, burning his passport and other personal papers. Handcuffs were found in his car, together with a bizarre ransom note addressed to the Queen. Had he managed to kidnap her daughter, he would have wanted £2 million, all in £5 notes, to guarantee her safe return. He stipulated that the cash should be placed in 20 unlocked suitcases and put on board a plane to Switzerland. At his trial in May, Ball was charged with attempted murder and kidnapping. He pleaded guilty. He had a history of mental illness and it was clear that he was seriously unwell. In one statement, he even claimed that his inability to get proper treatment for his psychiatric problems was the motivating force behind his kidnap attempt. 'I would like to say that I did it,' he said, 'because I wished to draw attention to the lack of facilities for treating mental illness under the National Health Service.' He was sentenced to life inside a secure facility and has served at least some of that time in Broadmoor.

Some days after the attempted kidnapping, a group calling itself the Marxist-Leninist Activist Revolutionary Movement sent a letter to the *Times*, claiming it was responsible for the attack, but there has never been a shred of evidence that anyone other than Ball was involved. As the Home Secretary Roy Jenkins reported to the House of Commons, 'There is no... indication that this was other than an isolated act by an individual'. The wounded men –

Beaton, Callender, Hills and McConnell – all spent time in hospital but recovered from their injuries. Beaton was awarded the George Cross for his bravery, Hills and Russell received the George Medal and Callender, McConnell and Edmonds the Queen's Gallantry Medal.

Terracotta Army

On 29 March 1974, six brothers named Yang, all in their forties and fifties, began to dig a new well on land in Shaanxi province, China. The area had been hit by a drought and they were concerned about the lack of water for their persimmon and pomegranate trees. As they drove their spades into the ground, in search of the precious liquid, they began to find fragments of pottery, useless for their needs. They continued to dig and, to their shock and alarm, a head appeared out of the earth. After a brief period of panic, they realised that it was made of terracotta. Was this an image of an earth-god? Had they found the remains of an ancient temple? They couldn't be sure but their main concern was still their search for water. Digging deeper, they unearthed a selection of shattered limbs and torsos made from the same material. In their attempts to discover a new source of water for themselves, the brothers Yang had stumbled on one of the greatest archaeological finds of all time – the Terracotta Warriors.

The man who did most to bring the Terracotta Army to the world's attention was a self-taught archaeologist named Zhao Kangmin. At the time the Yang brothers were digging their well, Zhao was the curator (and sole employee) of a small museum in an area known as Lintong, close to the ancient capital city of Xi'an. In 1962, he had himself discovered three kneeling terracotta crossbowmen and suspected that they must be part of a larger group of figures, possibly connected to China's first emperor, but he had not the resources to mount any substantial dig. He was also unsure of the date of his crossbowmen. On 25 April, four weeks after the Yang brothers' discovery, rumours of it had reached the wider world. Zhao received a phone call, asking him to go and see what the farmers had found. 'I got on my bicycle,' he later recalled, 'and rode to the field. The Yangs were still at work there, digging their well. I saw seven or eight pieces – bits of legs, arms and two heads – lying near the well.'

Zhao's visit was to change his life and the lives of the locals. He found fragments of figures everywhere in the village. One old woman had taken a head home, placed it on a table, lit incense and taken to praying to it. Some bits and pieces were being used as children's toys. Zhao collected everything he could find and returned to his museum where he began the elaborate job of piecing them all together. Not only was the discovery itself a chance one. So too was the way in which word of it spread. Had Zhao not arrived in the Yang brothers' village, it is entirely possible that the terracotta army would have remained hidden. 'The farmers would have destroyed the figures, because they thought they were unlucky things,' Zhao said later. 'They would have abandoned the well, and no one would have told the authorities.'

Initially, Zhao himself kept quiet about the warriors he had managed to reconstruct. He had his own experience of

Maoist vandalism during the so-called Cultural Revolution when Red Guards, contemptuous of the past, had smashed a statue in his own museum. He worried that the same fate might await his rebuilt figures. When a journalist from Beijing arrived in Lintong, visiting relatives, and saw the warriors, Zhao begged him not to write about them. On his return to the capital, the journalist took no notice of Zhao's plea and Chinese government officials were soon aware of what had been found. Thankfully, Zhao's fears proved unfounded. Instead of ordering the figures' destruction as worthless relics of a distant and ideologically unsound past, the authorities recognised their potential significance. A large-scale expedition was mounted to excavate the area around the initial find. Within a few months, excavations had begun on two further sites and hundreds more terracotta warriors had been discovered.

Today many thousands of the figures have been revealed and it is thought that there could be many thousands more still waiting to be unearthed. Each one is different, with unique physical features, and they wear appropriate uniforms for a variety of roles from infantryman to archer and cavalryman to charioteer. Originally painted in bright colours which have faded and flaked off over the centuries, and through exposure to the air, they are all part of an 'army' which also includes 140 battle chariots and nearly 700 horses. Arguably the strangest fact about the warriors is that they were never meant to be seen by ordinary human beings, certainly not by the millions who have travelled to Shaanxi province to look at them in the fifty years since the Yang brothers made their extraordinary find. The life-size figures were buried beneath the ground to act as an army after death for the First Qin Emperor, Qin Shi Huang, the man who, in the 3rd century BCE, turned a bunch of perpetually warring states into something like the single nation China is today. The Terracotta Army guards the Qin Emperor's enormous tomb and they stand ready for action in the afterlife to protect him.

April

The French president dies in office and in West Germany the chancellor is forced to resign in response to a spy scandal. Portugal sees a largely bloodless revolution in which the fascist Estado Novo regime is overthrown. In San Francisco the kidnapped heiress to a fortune is filmed taking part in an armed bank robbery. The Swedish supergroup Abba begin their journey to worldwide stardom with victory in the Eurovision Song Contest. Stephen King publishes his first novel. Manchester United suffer relegation from the first tier of English football.

Death in Office of Georges Pompidou

On 2 April the serving president of France, Georges Pompidou, died at his apartment in a building on the Île-Saint-Louis in Paris. He was 62 years old. He was born in 1911, the son of two teachers, in Montboudif, a small commune in the Cantal *département* of central France. After graduating from the prestigious École Normale Supérieure, his early career was as a teacher of literature in a Parisian lycée. A lieutenant during the Second World War, he won the Croix de Guerre, an award for outstanding bravery. Towards the end of the war, he came to the attention of Charles de Gaulle, then head of the provisional French government, who saw something in the young teacher turned soldier. Although he was a complete political novice, Pompidou became one of de Gaulle's protégés, working on his personal staff in the years immediately after the war.

In 1955, with de Gaulle in the middle of a long period out of power, Pompidou joined the Rothschild Bank in Paris and swiftly rose to become its director-general. When de Gaulle returned as president of the newly founded Fifth French Republic in 1958, Pompidou became his chief personal assistant and played a leading role in the drafting of a constitution for the new republic. He was also involved in the secret negotiations that finally brought to an end the bitter and protracted war between France and the Algerian National Liberation Front. De Gaulle appointed the relatively unknown Pompidou as prime minister in April 1962 and he went on to hold the post for more than six years.

Pompidou was himself elected as president of France in June 1969. His fellow Gaullist Jacques Chirac, a future French president himself, worked closely with Pompidou in the 1960s and 1970s, and later summed up his character in his memoirs. 'The man gave the appearance of being secretive, wily, a little cunning,' Chirac wrote, 'which he was, to a degree. However, it was primarily his intelligence, culture, and competence that conferred indisputable authority on him and commanded respect.' By 1973, it was his health rather than anything else that was of concern to political insiders in France.

Throughout much of that year, the government struggled to keep the president's recurring illnesses a secret but it proved impossible to do so. Few people believed the regular reports that he was suffering from colds or other minor ailments when the evidence of his deteriorating condition could be seen in his public appearances. He had put on weight, was often unsteady in his gait and his persistent tiredness was all too obvious. Despite this, he retained his popularity. In a poll conducted at the end of 1973, more than 55 per cent of those asked declared themselves satisfied with his presidency, although an even higher percentage thought that the overall problems in government were getting worse.

By the beginning of 1974, his ill-health was no longer any kind of a secret, and newspapers such as *L'Express* and *Le Monde* were debating the future of his government and the possibility that he might resign. At a rally for the Gaullist faithful at the end of January, he seemed barely able to stand. In February, it was officially announced that he had been forced to take to his bed during a particularly debilitating bout of flu. 'He's sick, very sick,' one observer concluded. 'It's no longer an unmentionable subject.' He was, in fact, suffering from a rare form of blood cancer known as Waldenström's disease and he died of it at the beginning of April.

The memorial service took place on 6 April in Notre-Dame Cathedral and was attended by a host of heads of state and other international dignitaries, including Richard Nixon, the British prime minister, Harold Wilson, Queen Juliana of the Netherlands, the Ethiopian emperor, Haile Selassie, and Willy Brandt, the chancellor of West Germany. Today Pompidou's name is best remembered, certainly outside France, through the Pompidou Centre, one of Paris's most visited tourist attractions. One of the projects the culture-loving president had championed during his time in office was the building of a modern art museum. After his death, the project was completed and named in his honour. In the presidential elections which followed Pompidou's death, Valéry Giscard d'Estaing beat Francois Mitterand and took office at the end of May.

Abba Win the Eurovision Song Contest

Who would stage the 1974 Eurovision Song Contest? The tradition established over the competition's first 18 years was that the country which provided the previous year's winner would host the next one but Luxembourg, which won in 1973, declined the chance to do so, claiming it was too costly. Instead the event was organised by the BBC and it took place in the Brighton Dome on 6 April. Seventeen countries sent singers or bands to compete for the glory of winning. (In comparison, 37 countries took part in the 2023 contest.) France withdrew at the last minute because of the death a few days earlier of its president, Georges Pompidou. When all the votes were counted there was an undisputed winner.

The Italian Gigliola Cinquetti had claimed second place with the song 'Si', gaining 18 points; the improbably named duo of Mouth and MacNeal (real names Willem Duyn and Sjoukje van't Spijker) from the Netherlands were placed third with 15 points; and Olivia Newton-John, performing for the UK and singing 'Long Live Love', was one of three contestants who tied for fourth on 14 points. At the top, with 24 points, was a Swedish group consisting of pianist Benny Andersson, guitarist Björn Ulvaeus and two glamorous female singers, blonde Agnetha Fältskog and brunette Anni-Frid Lyngstad. They were, of course, Abba.

The group had been formed in Stockholm two years earlier and had already attempted to achieve Eurovision glory in two previous years via the songs 'Better to Have Loved' (1972) and 'Ring Ring' (1973). Neither of these two compositions by Benny and Björn had made it beyond the Swedish selection stage of the Eurovision, although the latter went on to be a chart success in several European countries. However, 1974 was to be Abba's year. After briefly considering submitting a song entitled 'Hasta Mañana', they settled (wisely, with hindsight) on the extraordinarily catchy 'Waterloo', written by Benny and Björn and the group's manager Stig Anderson. At the Melodifestivalen in February, the contest to choose the Swedish entry for Eurovision, it was a runaway winner.

At Brighton two months later, they led the voting from start to finish, and went on to become the most popular and successful act ever to perform at Eurovision. Their previous attempts to qualify for the contest may have ended in failure but 'Waterloo' proved an enormous hit. From the moment the conductor, Sven-Olof Walldoff, appeared, dressed as Napoleon, both the live audience and millions watching on TV were on their side. 'Only two things will survive a nuclear apocalypse,' the journalist James Rampton wrote recently, 'cockroaches and our undying love for Abba.' For many people around Europe, and indeed around the world, that undying love began on an April night in Brighton in 1974.

A Spy in West Berlin

In 1974, Germany was still a divided country and its once and future capital, Berlin, was a divided city. This was still what might be called the 'Golden Age' of Cold War espionage. Both sides spied on each other. The legendary East German spymaster Markus Wolf, known for many years as 'The Man Without a Face' because authorities in the West did not even possess a fully authenticated photo of him, was head of the foreign intelligence division of the Ministry of State Security, the 'Stasi', for decades. During that time, he oversaw a succession of operations against the West. His greatest coup was to infiltrate an agent into the very heart of the West German government. Unbeknown to his counterparts in the West, one of Wolf's most successful spies for many years was a close aide to West Germany's Chancellor, Willy Brandt.

Günter Guillaume was born in Prenzlauer Berg, Berlin in February 1927, the son of a cinema pianist and a hairdresser. His father joined the Nazi Party soon after Hitler took power in Germany and Günter was himself a party member in the last year of the war. As a teenager in 1944, he was also conscripted into the German Air Force, working as a *Luftwaffenhelfer* or auxiliary. After the war he lived in East Germany and had a number of different jobs before he was recruited by the Stasi. At the age of 29, he and his wife Christel were instructed by their handlers to move to West Germany and to become involved in politics there. Claiming to be refugees from a system which denied them the freedom they wanted, they were accepted in the West. They settled in Frankfurt and initially ran a coffee shop in the city. They joined the Social Democratic Party of Germany (*Sozialdemokratische Partei Deutschlands*) there in late 1957. Günter rose through the ranks as a party functionary and joined the *Bundeskanzleramt* (Office of the Federal Chancellor) in Bonn in 1960.

His initial responsibilities involved liaison with trade unions. By 1972, his steadiness and willingness to work long hours had gained him a promotion. He was made one of Willy Brandt's three personal assistants.

The security services in Bonn began to have their suspicions about Guillaume as early as 1973 but they chose, for reasons which are not entirely clear, not to pursue them. They did not even warn Brandt in the summer of that year when the chancellor proposed taking Guillaume with him as his sole aide on a trip to Norway. The spy later confessed that this provided an opportunity for him to hand over copies of an array of top secret letters to his East German contacts, including ones from Brandt to the American president, Richard Nixon, in which he discussed NATO's nuclear strategy.

The West German security services finally made their move the following year and Guillaume was arrested on 24 April on his return from a holiday in the south of France. The news of the arrest was conveyed to Brandt at Bonn airport on the same day, after he had landed there following an official visit to Algeria and Egypt. When word reached the media, speculation in the tabloid press grew about the nature of the information Guillaume had transmitted to the GDR. Rumours even proliferated that the spy had also been a pimp, procuring women for the chancellor.

In his memoirs, Brandt was unsurprisingly eager to play down the role of the spy in his life. 'Guillaume was not someone who took part in political discussions,' he wrote, 'only a reliable aide; not a partner in serious conversation but a good, methodical worker... I did not especially like his company near me or for very long.' Nonetheless, it was the public exposure of an East German spy at the very heart of his government that was one of the main contributing factors to Brandt's downfall. Although the chancellor initially tried to ride out the storm, he had eventually to bow to the inevitable. Late on the evening of 6 May, he handed his letter of resignation to the Federal President, Gustav Heinemann. 'I take the political responsibility for negligence in connection with the spy affair Guillaume,' he said, 'and declare my resignation from the office of Federal Chancellor.' Ten days later, he was replaced by Helmut Schmidt, Minister of Finance in his government for the previous two years.

In late 1975, some 18 months after his exposure as a spy, Guillaume was sentenced to 13 years in prison, his wife to 8. They were both released from prison in 1981, in an exchange for Western spies held on the other side of the Berlin Wall. Returning to East Germany after 25 years away, the couple found it difficult to adjust to a society from which they had so long been absent. They divorced soon after their return. Although Guillaume was hailed as a national hero and was decorated with the Order of Karl Marx by the East German leader, Erich Honecker, he remained uncomfortable in the country for which he had engaged in high-level espionage. He took up a job training other, younger spies. He died of a heart attack in 1995.

The 'Guillaume Affair' has continued to fascinate people in the twenty-first century. Michael Frayn's play *Democracy*, first performed at London's National Theatre in 2003 and starring Roger Allam as the chancellor and Conleth Hill as his aide, focuses on it and the ambivalent relationship between the two men. In the same year, Willy Brandt's son, Matthias, who had become an actor, played the part, not of his father, as might have been expected, but of Guillaume in a TV film about the spy. Perhaps the greatest irony in the saga is that Markus Wolf later said that it had never been his intention to bring down Brandt and that the Guillaume Affair constituted one of the Stasi's biggest mistakes.

Patty Hearst in San Francisco Bank Raid

One of the most memorable photos of the 1970s is a grainy image of a dark-haired young woman clutching a machine gun. It was taken by a bank's security camera on 15 April and the woman was 20-year-old Patricia Hearst, the granddaughter of the newspaper tycoon William Randolph Hearst, supposedly the model for Charles Foster Kane, the protagonist of Orson Welles's 1941 film *Citizen Kane*. Just over two months earlier, Patty Hearst had been a student at the University of California, Berkeley, reading art history. On 4 February she was sitting in her apartment with her boyfriend, Steven Weed, when there was a knock on the door. They answered it to find a young woman claiming to have had a car accident and asking to use their phone. As they opened the door to her, two men with guns, who had been standing behind the visitor, pushed past them and into the apartment. One punched Weed to the floor and knocked him unconscious. Hearst was grabbed, bound with nylon cord and blindfolded. A neighbour, hearing the fracas, arrived to see what was happening. He was also knocked to the ground and tied up. Steven Weed, coming round, saw a chance to escape and fled out of the back door. Patty Hearst was bundled down the stairs from the apartment and into the boot of a car. She was being kidnapped by a group of left-wing activists who called themselves the Symbionese Liberation Army (SLA).

In their manifesto, the founders of the SLA, Donald DeFreeze and Patricia Soltysik, explained that, 'The name "symbionese" is taken from the word "symbiosis" and we define its meaning as a body of dissimilar bodies and organisms living in deep and loving harmony and partnership in the best interest of all within the body'. The group never consisted of more than a handful of individuals who could all, in the words of one writer, 'fit inside a Chevy van'. Unfortunately, in pursuit of 'deep and loving harmony and partnership', the SLA engaged in murder, kidnapping and bank robbery.

They had kidnapped Patty, they claimed, as a punishment for 'crimes her mother and father have committed against we the American people and the oppressed people of the world'. Their first demand arrived in a message warning that Patty would be killed should any attempt be made to rescue her and ending in the SLA's catchy motto, 'Death to the Fascist Insect That Preys Upon the Life of the People'. The Hearst family was told it should use its influence to persuade the state of California to release two SLA members who had been arrested in connection with the killing of a prominent educationalist the previous November. As was made immediately clear, this was never going to happen. There was no possibility that the authorities in California would release suspected killers to please the Hearst family.

The SLA's next proposal was that the Hearsts should distribute food to the poor of California. On 22 February, Patty's father arranged the first distribution in the Bay Area but, as might perhaps have been predicted, chaos ensued. Long queues formed at the distribution points and fighting broke out at some of these between would-be recipients and the police. In Oakland, organisers were reduced to throwing food from a window to a crowd of several thousands below. One man was knocked unconscious and people began to hurl tins of food back. Some of those who qualified for the handouts refused to accept them, feeling they were tainted by association with the SLA. 'I value human life a little higher than a bag of groceries,' one person said.

During all this time Patty Hearst was being held by the SLA and subjected to an array of physical and mental torments. Locked in a small room, blindfolded and with her hands tied, she was regularly threatened with death. At her trial, it was stated that she was also raped by DeFreeze and others. Intermittently, she was released and allowed to participate in the group discussions of politics, society and revolution. Her ideas about her kidnappers began to change. Over the next weeks, the SLA sent a series of audiotapes to the Hearst family in which Patty's voice was heard, sounding increasingly sympathetic to the group's beliefs. Finally, on 3 April, she said, 'I have been given the choice of being released... or joining the forces of the Symbionese Liberation Army and fighting for my freedom and the freedom of all oppressed people. I have chosen to stay and fight.' In her new incarnation as a freedom fighter, she took the name 'Tania' in reference to the *nom de guerre* of Haydée Tamara Bunke Bider, who had fought alongside the revolutionary Che Guevara in the jungles of Bolivia, and had died there seven years earlier.

Twelve days later, members of the SLA, including Hearst, entered the Hibernia Bank at 1450 Noriega Street, San Francisco, brandishing weapons. One of them, Nancy Ling Perry, was so nervous that she dropped her ammunition clip with a clatter and had to bend down to retrieve it. Their leader, Donald DeFreeze, pushed past her and yelled at the eighteen employees and six customers in the building that morning. 'This is a holdup!' he roared. 'The first motherf--er who don't lay down on the floor gets shot in the head!' As people obeyed his orders, another SLA member vaulted the partition dividing staff from customers and began to grab the money from the cash drawers. Patty Hearst had been ordered by DeFreeze to make her presence known by standing in full view of the security cameras and shooting a round into the bank's ceiling. As it was, her gun jammed at the vital moment and all she was able to do was to shout, 'This is Tania... Patricia Hearst', before joining her new comrades in guarding the people lying on the ground.

Despite the problem with Patty's gun, the raid was going more or less to plan but it began to unravel when two new customers walked into the bank. Pete Markoff and Gene Brennan were completely unaware of what was going on. Nancy Ling Perry panicked once again and shot at them, hitting Brennan in the hand and Markoff in the buttocks. Bleeding, both men stumbled back on to the pavement outside. Inside the bank, it was obviously time for the SLA to retreat with whatever loot they had managed to seize. Stepping over Markoff who had slumped to the ground, they ran for their getaway car and left.

Argument now raged in the media and elsewhere over Patty's involvement in the bank robbery. Was she a willing participant? Or had she been brainwashed into taking her place alongside the other armed robbers? In another audiotape, she pooh-poohed the latter idea as 'ridiculous beyond belief'. She was, she announced, 'a soldier in the People's Army'. Another month passed before Patty was again seen. At a sporting goods store in Inglewood, California, shots were fired when an attempt was made to detain a suspected shoplifter. The shoplifter was William Harris, an SLA member, and the gunwoman, sitting in a vehicle outside, who peppered the store's sign with semi-automatic rifle fire, was Patty Hearst. She and Harris and Harris's wife, Emily, fled the scene in a Volkswagen van, later found abandoned. Inside its glove box, the police found evidence which led them to an SLA 'safe' house in East 54th Street, Los Angeles.

On 17 May, police officers and SWAT teams surrounded the house. Patty and the Harrises were not there but Donald DeFreeze and five of his SLA comrades were. Heavily armed, they were in no mood to surrender. The ensuing shootout took place in front of a live nationwide TV audience. This audience included Patty and the Harrises who were holed up in a hotel not far away and watched in horror as events unfolded. Two of the SLA members were shot dead as they ran from the house, firing off their weapons. The others died inside, either from gunshot wounds or the effects of smoke inhalation from the fire which had broken out during the battle. Donald DeFreeze is assumed to have turned his gun on himself rather than be captured.

Shocked by what they had seen of the deaths of their comrades, Patty Hearst and the Harrises decided to leave the West Coast and they spent the autumn of 1974 in hiding in Pennsylvania. For nearly a year after that they crisscrossed America, surviving on the proceeds of a series of robberies. During one of these heists, at the Crocker

National Bank in Carmichael, California, a mother of four named Myrna Opsahl was shot dead. Patty was the getaway driver. Patty Hearst, aka Tania, was finally arrested in San Francisco on 18 September 1975. When asked her occupation as she was being booked into jail, she said, 'Urban Guerrilla'. She went on trial the following January, charged with bank robbery, and was found guilty. Originally given a sentence of 35 years, she was released in February 1979 after President Jimmy Carter commuted her sentence. It was not until Bill Clinton, in one of the last acts of his presidency, granted her a full pardon in 2001 that she was finally exonerated. Arguments about the extent and nature of her culpability in the dramatic events of 1974 continue. Was she an entirely willing participant in them? Or was she an extreme example of so-called Stockholm Syndrome in which hostages or kidnap victims form a strong psychological bond with those holding them?

Carnation Revolution

By 1974, the Estado Novo regime had been in power in Portugal for more than four decades. Between 1932 and 1968, the country had been ruled by Antonio Salazar as prime minister and virtual dictator. Illness forced Salazar to step down and he died in 1970. His successor as prime minister, Marcelo Caetano, faced problems on many fronts. At home, the country's finances were in a mess. In Africa, their colonial wars, fought as Angola and Mozambique struggled to gain independence, were not going well and were a drain on the country's resources. The military, on whom the regime ultimately depended for its survival, was growing increasingly restive and unhappy. Many of the officers were disgusted with Caetano's insistence on pouring men and money into the wars against pro-independence guerrillas in the African colonies. Losses in these faraway conflicts had been high – more than 9,000 young Portuguese soldiers dead and at least another 25,000 wounded – and no end to them was in sight.

Early in 1974, a veteran of the African wars, General Antonio Spinola, published a book entitled *Portugal and the Future*. He sent a copy to Caetano who read it with a sense of impending doom. 'As I closed it,' the prime minister later confessed, 'I understood that a *coup d'état*, the approach of which I had felt for months, was now inevitable.' The first attempt at one proved something of a damp squib. Several hundred officers had already joined together to create the *Movimento das Forças Armadas* ('Armed Forces Movement') and, in March 1974, there was a minor revolt by officers and men stationed in the provincial city of Caldas. They marched on Lisbon, intending to occupy the airport but this ill-planned coup fizzled out when they realised that no other army units were joining them. They turned back to their barracks at Caldas where they were swiftly arrested and imprisoned in military jails. (They would be released in just over a month's time.)

However, the regime had merely postponed rather than prevented its downfall. On 25 April two songs became the signals for renewed attempts to overthrow the Estado Novo. In the Eurovision Song Contest held in Brighton earlier in the month, Paulo de Carvalho had performed 'E Depois do Adeus' as Portugal's entry. The song had been met with little approval and had finished joint last with only three votes cast in its favour. Now it had a central role to play in an unfolding drama. When it was aired on national radio at 10.55am that day, it alerted rebel soldiers that the coup was to begin. At 12.20am the following day, the playing of another song, 'Grândola, Vila Morena', written by José Afonso, a musician renowned for his opposition to the regime, gave the green light to all the dissident soldiers.

Tanks now rolled into the centre of Lisbon. The main bridge over the city's river, the Tagus, was seized by rebel troops and the airport and the most important television station were also soon under their control. Caetano and other ministers, hearing news of the rebels' successes, took refuge in a barracks but soldiers stormed the place and arrested them. It was soon clear that the existing Novo Estado government had lost the will to fight against what seemed inevitable. As one historian has noted, 'In less than twenty hours a regime that had lasted nearly half a century...collapsed'. Caetano and other ministers were despatched to Madeira en route to exile in Brazil. The deposed prime minister's chief complaint seemed to be that the soldiers sent to escort him were commanded by a mere sergeant-major. It is not true that the April revolution was entirely bloodless. At one point on the 25th the old regime's political police opened fire on a crowd of demonstrators and four were killed. However, these were the only deaths in what proved to be a remarkably peaceful coup.

Why did the events surrounding the overthrow of the Estado Novo regime come to be known as the 'Carnation Revolution'? It was largely because of the actions of a woman in her early forties named Celeste Caeiro who was working in a Lisbon restaurant that was about to celebrate its first anniversary. The plan was that, on 25 April, she and other staff would hand out flowers to their customers. Events overtook them and, because of the coup, the idea was abandoned. The restaurant closed for the day and Caeiro was told she could do as she wished with the red and white carnations that had been bought for the cancelled celebration. On her way home, she encountered groups of soldiers on the streets and one of them asked her for a cigarette. She replied that she didn't smoke but, in a moment of inspiration, she offered him a carnation instead. The soldier accepted the flower and placed it in the muzzle of his gun. It was a symbolic gesture which led Caeiro to distribute the rest of the carnations to his comrades who followed his example. The idea quickly caught on. Other people bought more flowers to distribute to the soldiers and soon red and white carnations were everywhere in the streets of Lisbon.

Stephen King's First Novel

1974 was the year the writer Stephen King's life took a dramatic turn for the better. Since graduating from the University of Maine four years earlier with a degree in English, he had had short stories published in various magazines but they had not earned him enough money to allow him to concentrate on his writing. His main income was from his work as a high school teacher in the small town of Hampden, Maine. All this was to change after he started to think about a plot involving a high-school girl with unexpected powers.

King's original intention was to produce a short story for the magazine *Cavalier* which had already published several of his stories. He hit difficulties almost immediately. The opening scene was to include the unexpected onset of the central character's first period. King later wrote, 'As I arrived at this... I suddenly realized that I 1) had never been a girl, 2) had never had a... menstrual period, 3) had absolutely no idea how I'd react to one'. Faced with this problem, his instinct was to ditch the story but his wife, Tabitha, persuaded him to persist with it. He followed her advice, not least because, as he recalled decades later, 'I was dry and had no better ideas'. Expanded into a novel-length manuscript, *Carrie* won King a contract with the publisher Doubleday and it appeared on the shelves of American bookshops on 5 April 1974. The story of an alienated teenage girl, bullied at school, who takes revenge on her tormentors after she discovers (or rediscovers) that she has telekinetic powers, it proved a bestseller in its paperback edition and a pivotal work in the genre of horror literature. In the words of the writer and critic Jeff VanderMeer, '*Carrie* changed the paradigm by announcing a very American form of horror that broke with the past'.

King was able to give up his day job as a teacher and work full-time as a writer. He was launched on a career which has seen him become one of the most commercially successful authors of the last half-century. His books have sold in their millions. Dozens of films have been made from his works. Brian De Palma's film version of *Carrie*, which was released in 1976 and starred Sissy Spacek as the title character, was a box-office triumph, costing less than $2 million to make and taking $33 million in North America alone. It has been regularly hailed as one of the finest horror movies of all time. A remake, less universally acclaimed, appeared in 2013. Although the story may not immediately suggest that it had the potential to be turned into a musical, it has also been adapted into exactly that. Perhaps unsurprisingly, the show was not a success in its original 1988 Broadway production (it closed after only five performances) but it has been revived several times this century. *Carrie* was the making of Stephen King and, had Doubleday not seen its potential and agreed to publish it, the world might never have seen later horror masterpieces such as *Salem's Lot*, *It* and *The Shining*.

Manchester United Relegated

Today, Manchester United is one of the most famous names in world football. Despite recent tribulations, it remains the English club with the most league titles (20) to its credit. It seems almost inconceivable that the team could be relegated from the top flight of English football but that is precisely what happened at the end of the 1973-74 season.

Their legendary manager Matt Busby, who had put together the 'Busby Babes' team and then rebuilt the side after so many of them had died in the Munich air disaster of 1958, had retired in 1969. He handed over the reins to the 31-year-old Wilf McGuinness, the reserve team manager. A period of turmoil followed. McGuinness was eventually sacked, and Busby returned as interim manager before Frank O'Farrell was appointed in June 1971 and took over the role at the beginning of July. Success of the kind that United fans expected eluded O'Farrell and he was replaced by Tommy Docherty in December 1972, with the club perilously close to the bottom of the First Division, then the top level of English football. Docherty steered them to survival but the club was in decline. Aging stars like Bobby Charlton and Denis Law left. George Best, already firmly embarked on his campaign to destroy his own talent and thumb his nose at all those who admired him, was at loggerheads with his manager, his fellow players and, it sometimes seemed, the world. The omens for the 1973-74 season were not good.

United began well enough but, between September 1973 and March 1974, they recorded only four wins in twenty matches. For a brief period in April, it looked as if the team was rallying. They won three games on the trot but, as the season neared its end, they were still firmly in the relegation zone. Their last home game, on 27 April, was against their rivals from Maine Road, Manchester City. United needed a draw at the very least to maintain any chance of staying up. As the game headed into its final ten minutes, it was still 0-0. However, in the 81st minute, City took the lead when one of their strikers backheeled the ball into the net. By a terrible irony, the goalscorer was Denis Law, one of the stars of United's not so distant glory years, who had joined City on a free transfer at the beginning of the season. Law did not celebrate his goal. He simply stood, in the words of the sports writer David Goldblatt, 'his arms frozen by his side, rigid and unemotive' as he was 'mobbed by his new team-mates'. The reaction of fans was more dramatic. A series of pitch invasions forced the referee into abandoning the game in the 85th minute, although the Football Association later ruled that the result, 1-0 to City, should stand. It has often been said that City's victory was what sent their rivals into the Second Division. In some kind of symbolic sense, this is true enough but, had fellow strugglers Birmingham City and West Ham not beaten Norwich and drawn with Liverpool respectively, United might have escaped their fate. As it was, these two results meant that they could not hope to catch the teams above them, no matter how well they did in their final match. In the event, they lost 1-0 to Stoke City.

It was only six years since they had won the European Cup, now the Champions League, beating Benfica 4-1 and becoming the first English side to do so, but United would play the next season in the Second Division. Despite the relegation, the club kept faith in Tommy Docherty as manager and he repaid it by returning United to the top flight in the following season. They have played there ever since.

May

Sir Alf Ramsey, who had led his team to victory in the 1966 World Cup, is sacked as England's football manager. Italians are invited to vote in a referendum on the divisive subject of divorce. Legendary American band leader Duke Ellington dies in New York. David Bowie releases his Diamond Dogs album. In Israel, three Palestinian terrorists kill 25 of the hostages, many of them children, they have taken in the town of Ma'alot. India tests a nuclear weapon. In South Africa, the British Lions rugby union team begin what is to be their unbeaten tour of the country.

Sacking of Alf Ramsey

As manager of the England football team in 1974, Sir Alf Ramsey had a lot of credit in the bank. He had, after all, led his side to victory in the 1966 World Cup, a feat that no English manager has been able to repeat since. He had gone on to take them to the 1970 Mexico World Cup as defending champions and, although they had lost 3-2 to West Germany in the quarter-final (after leading 2-0 at one point), they had not disgraced themselves. At times they had played very well, particularly in their narrow 1-0 defeat to Pele's Brazil, often claimed to be the finest ever international side.

However, by 1973, even that credit was running out. A 2-0 defeat to Poland in June in a World Cup qualifier was seen as a particularly low point. By the time the return fixture was played at Wembley on 17 October, England needed a victory to send them to West Germany for the World Cup finals the following year. Despite recent setbacks, it seemed more likely than not that they would get it. Before the match, former Derby County manager and mouthy TV pundit, Brian Clough, had assured viewers that the Polish goalkeeper, Jan Tomaszewski, was a 'clown'. The 'clown' proceeded to play the game of his life, saving shot after shot that looked destined for the back of the net. The final score was 1-1. England, under Sir Alf Ramsey, had failed to qualify. They had, in the words of one journalist, been 'relegated to a place among soccer's second-class powers'.

As a result of that Wembley night, Ramsey was doomed to the sack. The only debate would be over its timing. The truth was that Ramsey looked like a man out of his times.

(To be fair, he looked like a man out of his times even in the 1960s, the decade of his greatest triumph. The 1950s, the years in which he had played for England himself as a right-back, seemed the era to which he was best suited.) He was a deeply conservative, buttoned-up individual with little discernible sense of humour and a slightly pompous, unnatural way of expressing himself. (Intent on self-improvement, he had taken elocution lessons which, in the words of one obituarist, 'had stranded his vowels halfway to Mayfair'.) Few things reveal the widening gap between the conventional Ramsey and his more irreverent players in the 1970s better than the often-told and possibly apocryphal story of his exchange with Rodney Marsh. Ramsey warned the mercurial forward before one international that he had to improve his work rate. 'If you don't,' he said, 'I'm going to pull you off at half-time.' 'Christ,' Marsh is supposed to have replied. 'At Manchester City all we get at half-time is a cup of tea and an orange.'

Although the decision to sack him had been made weeks earlier, and Ramsey had been told at the time, the public announcement was delayed until 1 May 1974. He left after taking charge in 113 matches of which he had won 69 and only lost 17. The sacking was a deeply traumatic experience for him. 'It was the most devastating half-hour of my life,' he once said of it. 'I stood in a room almost full of staring committee men. It was just like I was on trial. I thought I was going to be hanged.' His caretaker replacement was Joe Mercer, former manager of Manchester City. Mercer was not entirely keen on the task he had been given. According to some reports, his first words to the England squad of players were, 'I didn't want this bloody job in the first place'. On a more permanent basis, the bloody job went to Don Revie, the Leeds United manager, who was offered a salary more than twice that Sir Alf had been paid. Revie lasted three years, managing the national side for 29 matches without any outstanding success, before making the controversial decision to leave for an even better paid job as manager of the United Arab Emirates.

Apart from a brief, and not wildly successful, period in charge of Birmingham City in 1977-8, and a year in Greece as technical director of the Athens club Panathinaikos, his England sacking saw the end of Ramsey's managerial career. More than two decades after his death in 1999, he remains England's greatest manager. His sacking, however justified in retrospect, was not handled well. As Alan Ball, one of the World Cup-winning side, later said, with forgivable hyperbole, the treatment of Sir Alf, was 'the most incredible thing that ever happened in English football'. The man who guided his team to victory in the World Cup was unceremoniously ejected from the job he had held for 11 years with a meagre payoff of £8,000 and an annual pension of just over £1,000.

Italian Divorce Referendum

In what was still a predominantly Catholic society, divorce was a controversial subject in Italy and it became one of the country's most pressing and divisive issues in the late 1960s and early 1970s. The right for the state to allow a marriage to be dissolved was first proposed by a socialist politician, Loris Fortuna, in 1965 and was met with howls of outrage and dismay from traditionalists. However, history was against them and Fortuna gathered increasing support over the next few years. In November 1969, the Italian parliament voted by 325 to 283 in favour of state-sanctioned divorce and the so-called *Legge Fortuna* became law in December of the following year. This was the first time that divorce was permitted since the country was unified. (Divorce had been briefly allowed in parts of Italy under the rule of Napoleon.)

The *Legge Fortuna* remained highly controversial and campaigns to have it repealed had attracted significant support. Signatures were sought on a petition to get rid of the law and, within six months, a million people put their names to it. The Italian constitution stated that only half a million signatures were needed to oblige the government to hold a referendum on the possible repeal of a law so, on 12-13 May 1974, a vote was held to discover what the majority of Italians wanted. The question asked was whether or not you wanted the law abrogated. If you voted 'Yes', you were voting for a return to the time when divorce was illegal; if you voted 'No' you were voting for the law to remain and for divorce to be a legal right.

Pope Paul VI maintained an official silence on the issue, although he had already expressed his 'deep grief' when the divorce law had been originally passed and, by exhorting a crowd gathered in St Peter's Square on the first day of the referendum to pray to the Virgin Mary 'for the well-being of the family', he was making it perfectly clear how he believed Catholics should vote. The right-wing politician Amintore Fanfani, a past and future prime minister, had earlier sought to make political capital from the issue, launching a crusade against legal divorce. At one point, he claimed that allowing it was but the first step on the road to sexual anarchy and that, before Italians knew it, there would be such things as homosexual marriage.

Italy's entry for the Eurovision Song Contest in 1974 was, unfortunately, entitled 'Si', the Italian word for 'Yes'. Although Gigliola Cinquetti's song had nothing whatsoever to do with the referendum, and the competition was taking place a month before people were going to be asked to vote, RAI, the Italian state television channel, decided not to broadcast the Eurovision Contest, just in case some viewers might be subconsciously influenced by an attractive young woman singing the word 'Si' repeatedly. So most Italians were unable to see Gigliola come second in the competition to a Swedish group named Abba (see p. 76).

The debate aroused very strong feelings on both sides, a fact reflected in the high turnout on the two days of the referendum. More than 85 per cent of those eligible to vote did so. The result was a resounding victory for those who wanted to retain the new right to divorce: 59.26 per cent voted 'No'; 40.74 per cent 'Yes'.

Duke Ellington Dies

One of the greatest of all jazz composers died in New York of lung cancer and pneumonia on 24 May 1974, a month after his 75th birthday. Edward Kennedy Ellington was born in Washington DC in 1899. He had a comfortable, middle-class upbringing in which his early interest in music and playing the piano was encouraged. In his teenage years, his elegance and dapper dress sense persuaded friends to call him 'Duke' and the nickname stayed with him for the rest of his life. He put together his first band, The Duke's Serenaders, at this time and was playing in New York venues by 1923. Four years later, his ensemble became the house band at the legendary Cotton Club in Harlem. He began recording at much the same time, including such songs as 'East St Louis Toodle-Oo', and 'Creole Love Call', his own early compositions written in collaboration with the trumpet player Bubber Miley. In 1930, he wrote what was to become one of his most famous songs, 'Mood Indigo'.

From then until the last years of his life he created thousands of songs, suites and other musical pieces. His band's signature tune, 'Take the A Train', was written by Billy Strayhorn, the man who became his most frequent collaborator. ('Strayhorn does a lot of the work but I get to take the bows!' Ellington once joked.) Other great names in the history of jazz, from the saxophonists Johnny Hodges and Ben Webster to the clarinetist Barney Bigard and the trumpeter Ray Nance, played with Ellington's band. His ambitions for his music grew ever larger. *Black, Brown and Beige*, premiered at Carnegie Hall in 1943, was introduced by Ellington as 'a parallel to the history of the Negro in America' and was followed by large-scale pieces like *Such Sweet Thunder*, from 1957, based on themes from Shakespeare, and 1967's *Far East Suite*. In the last decade of his life Ellington also composed a number of religious works.

His funeral at the Cathedral of St John the Divine was attended by approximately 10,000 mourners crammed into the building itself and a further 2,500 who stood and listened to the service via loudspeaker in front of the Amsterdam Avenue entrance. Echoing words which the bandleader had often used himself at the end of his concerts, Reverend Norman O'Connor, a long-time friend of the composer, said, 'Duke, we thank you. You loved us madly. We will love you madly, today, tomorrow, and forever.' Ellington was buried at Woodlawn Cemetery in the Bronx, next to the graves of his parents. 'My men and my race are the inspiration of my work,' he once said. 'I try to catch the spirit and feeling of my people.'

David Bowie Releases Diamond Dogs

With his androgynous appearance and the deliberate theatricality of his music and his stage persona, David Bowie was one of the iconic cultural figures of the 1970s. In the two albums, *The Rise and Fall of Ziggy Stardust and the Spiders From Mars* (1972) and *Aladdin Sane* (1973), he had created and cultivated his Ziggy Stardust alter ego. By 1974, Bowie, restlessly imaginative and obsessed with shape-shifting and metamorphosis, was looking to move on from the Ziggy character. He had long been intrigued by George Orwell's *1984*. Bowie had even had hopes to adapt the book for the stage but Orwell's estate denied him the rights and he was obliged to forget the idea. He didn't forget his fascination with the idea of a dystopian future such as Orwell had imagined and it was reflected in his 1974 album, *Diamond Dogs*, which was issued by RCA in the UK on 24 May and went to number one in the UK Albums Chart. With its cover painting by the Belgian artist Guy Peellaert, depicting Bowie as half-man, half-dog, the album was visually distinctive and musically wide-ranging. The best known single taken from it is 'Rebel Rebel', which had been released earlier in the year and, if anything, feels like an adieu to his glam rock days but another single off the album, '1984', had been originally intended for the musical based on Orwell's novel he had once hoped to stage. The title track introduces a new addition to Bowie's repertoire of alter egos in Halloween Jack who lives on the top floor of an abandoned skyscraper in some post-apocalyptic version of New York.

In pursuit of his vision for *Diamond Dogs*, Bowie had got rid of many of the people who had contributed to the sound of his earlier albums. Gone was producer Ken Scott. Also absent was his backing group, the Spiders from Mars, including, most notably, the much-admired guitarist, Mick Ronson. Not everyone liked the new album on its first release. In *Rolling Stone*, Ken Emerson called it 'perhaps Bowie's worst album in six years' and claimed that he 'has deliberately cheapened himself and his music'. Like other commentators, Emerson missed Mick Ronson's presence. Why did Bowie choose to take Ronson's role of lead guitarist himself? It was, Emerson thought, 'like Mick Jagger filling in for Keith Richards'. However, with the passing of the years, the status of a work that one cultural commentator has described as 'wonderfully dark proto-punk' has only grown. In a *Guardian* review of a thirtieth-anniversary version, Adam Sweeting wrote, '*Diamond Dogs*, groaning under its conceptual baggage of mad-dog apocalypse, seemed vaguely unsatisfying on its release in 1974, but it emerges from this refurbished twin-disc edition as one of the most interesting episodes in Bowie's career'. And David Buckley, one of Bowie's biographers, has called it 'cinematic in scope, breathtakingly audacious in execution'.

India Tests a Nuclear Weapon

Given the innocuous-sounding code name of 'Operation Smiling Buddha', India's first successful test of a nuclear bomb was detonated on 18 May which, in 1974, was a festival day in India to mark Buddha's birthday. Nearly two years earlier, the country's prime minister Indira Gandhi had authorised scientists at the Bhabha Atomic Research Centre (BARC), named after Homi Jehangir Bhabha, often described as the 'father of the Indian nuclear programme', to proceed with making and testing a nuclear device. Work on it had proceeded apace. The two men most actively engaged in its creation were Raja Ramanna and PK Iyengar. Ramanna had succeeded Bhabha as the head of BARC's nuclear programme after the latter's untimely death in an air crash in 1966; Iyengar was another brilliant Indian physicist who had worked at the BARC since the 1950s. The test, which India repeatedly claimed at the time was for peaceful purposes only, took place at the Pokhran Test Range on the Rajasthan Steppe. After the successful underground detonation of the device, Ramanna put in a phone call to the Indian prime minister, Indira Gandhi, and told her, 'The Buddha has smiled'.

This was the first nuclear weapons test carried out by a country that wasn't one of the permanent members of the UN Security Council (USA, USSR, Britain, France and China). Within India itself it was greeted with pride and delight by many commentators and it had the effect of reviving Indira Gandhi's flagging popularity. Outside the country, the claims that the explosion of a nuclear bomb had been carried out with entirely peaceful intentions were met with scepticism. Few in the international community believed them. Certainly, Pakistan, which had been engaged in a military conflict with India only a few years earlier, did not. Its immediate response to Operation Smiling Buddha was to accelerate its own nuclear programme.

Condemnation was also swift to come from many in the international community. India did not carry out any further such tests until 1998.

Ma'alot Massacre

On a Sunday in May, three armed members of the PDF, the Popular Democratic Front (later known as the Democratic Front for the Liberation of Palestine), crossed the border from Lebanon into Israel, disguised as Israeli soldiers. After attacking a van, and shooting dead one of its passengers, they made their way towards the town of Ma'alot, six miles south of the Lebanese border. In the early hours of the morning they broke into a house belonging to the Cohen family and killed the mother, father and one of their children. Leaving the house as dawn approached, they headed for the Netiv Meir Elementary School which was being used as a hostel by teenagers from a high school in the town of Safed on a field trip in northern Israel. The three terrorists rapidly took control of the whole building, although some of the students and several teachers were able to escape by jumping out of a window. (The teachers were later pilloried in the press and elsewhere for what was seen as abandonment of their charges but they were cleared of wrongdoing by an enquiry.) The escapees alerted the local authorities and Golda Meir, then the country's prime minister, was soon apprised of what was happening. Moshe Dayan, the flamboyant minister of defence, flew to Ma'alot to take overall charge of the government response, arriving there soon after 7am.

By that time the terrorists, Hasan al-Atmah, Abdar-Rahim Ka'ik and Muhammad Salim Dardour, all Palestinian Arab men in their twenties, had made their demands known. They wanted more than twenty fellow members of the PDF released immediately from Israeli jails and put on a plane to Damascus, together with a Japanese national who had been involved two years earlier in a massacre at what is now Ben-Gurion Airport in Tel Aviv. Once they had conclusive proof that this had taken place, half the hostages would be freed. The others would be released after the hostage-takers had themselves been granted safe passage to the Syrian capital. If the terrorist demands were not met by that evening they would commence killing their hostages.

Dayan decided upon a twofold approach to the crisis. He arranged for Israel's most experienced and skilful hostage negotiator, Victor Cohen, to come to Ma'alot and engage with the terrorists. He also worked with military advisers to devise a plan to assault the building and neutralise the gunmen without precipitating the deaths of any of the hostages. Cohen succeeded in making contact but the preparations for any possible attack, which involved the arrival by helicopter of dozens of extra troops, spooked the three terrorists. Nervous, they began to shoot aimlessly through the windows. One of their shots hit and killed a soldier who was doing no more than observing the action from a distance.

Dayan was by now convinced that negotiation was pointless and that a military operation was required but Meir was reluctant to give it the go-ahead. It was only when attempts to act as intermediaries by various parties, including the French and Romanian ambassadors, became deadlocked that the government gave its approval to the armed rescue mission. At 5.45pm on 15 May, a mere quarter of an hour before the three terrorists had said they would kill their hostages if their demands were not met, Israeli special forces stormed the building. In the chaos, the assault went badly wrong. It could only have worked if the terrorists had been killed almost immediately and they were not. One of them, Rahim, although wounded in the shoulder, was able not only to direct automatic gunfire toward the hostages gathered together in the classroom but to pitch a grenade into their midst. Twenty-five were killed and others badly wounded. Rahim's gun then jammed and he was shot dead by Israeli soldiers. The other two terrorists, who had attempted to escape through a window, were also killed. The final death toll in the Ma'alot Massacre was

31 Israelis plus the three Palestinian gunmen. Reflecting on events years later, the commander of the special forces' attempt at rescue, said, 'The whole operation took 30, 35 seconds... If we'd been able to do it in 10, how many more could we have saved?'

The Israeli response to the massacre was immediate and ruthless. The very next day, aircraft were despatched to bomb what were believed to be offices and training bases for the PDF. Most of them were situated in refugee camps in southern Lebanon. The raids killed at least 27 people and dozens more were injured.

British and Irish Lions Begin Tour of South Africa

The announcement that the British and Irish Lions would tour South Africa in the summer of 1974 was unsurprisingly controversial from the beginning. This was, of course, during the apartheid years and criticism of the decision to play in the country was inevitable. Other sporting teams had already decided that they would not visit South Africa. Some of those who were likely to be picked for this tour were not keen to go. Two leading Welsh players, the flanker John Taylor and the wing Gerald Davies, made it known that they would not be available. Taylor had been picked for the previous Lions' tour of South Africa in 1968 and deeply regretted going. He had, he said many years later, been told that they were not supporting apartheid but building bridges. 'As soon as I got there I discovered what a load of nonsense that was. By the time I came back I knew I was not going to play against them again.' As for

Davies, he later said, 'I didn't feel I wanted to politicise it. It was a personal moral feeling I had... It was between myself and my conscience and I have never regretted that decision.'

Once the party arrived in South Africa, there was plenty of controversy on the pitch as well as off. The Lions were captained by the Irish lock forward Willie John McBride. He had toured the country before and knew that South African sides could be physically intimidating and were not averse to using such tactics as late tackling and deliberate foul play to unsettle opponents. He was determined that his team would not be cowed by on-pitch aggression which would be met with immediate retaliation. He devised the '99' call which he would shout out if there were trouble. (It was originally intended to be '999', as in the emergency phone number, but McBride found this was too long.) On hearing it, his team-mates would all go for the nearest opponent. In response to such a melee, the referee could scarcely send the whole team off and would have great difficulty singling out an individual to punish. McBride later said that the '99' call was only ever used once on the tour, thus sending out the successful message that the Lions would not be intimidated. However, the 1974 tour certainly saw some fearsome on-pitch violence. In the Third Test, the Scottish forward Gordon Brown tackled his opposite number, Johan de Bruyn, so hard that the latter's glass eye flew out. Play had to be stopped while the players of both sides, plus the referee, searched for the missing eye. 'Eventually someone yells "Eureka",' Brown recalled years later, 'whereupon de Bruyn grabs it and plonks it straight back in the gaping hole in his face'.

Despite the aggression and intimidation that marked it, the tour should also be remembered for its brilliant rugby. Playing under McBride's captaincy were such legendary figures as Gareth Edwards, Phil Bennett, JPR Williams and Mike Gibson, and the 1974 Lions are often described as the best British or Irish rugby team ever to tour abroad. They won 21 out of 22 games played and only missed out on a clean sweep of all their matches when they drew the last of their four Tests against the Springboks. Their opening match, against Western Transvaal, took place in the city of Potchefstroom on 15 May. The tourists finished easy winners, scoring 59 points to their opponents' 13. As the matches continued, with one played every few days throughout May, June and July, the tour became something of a triumphal march through South Africa. Game after game was won, some by huge margins. (They beat South West Districts 97-0 and ran out winners against Griqualand West by 69 points to 16.) The First Test against the international Springbok side was a much closer contest, finishing 12-3 to the visitors, but the Second and Third Tests were both very comfortable victories for the Lions, 28-9 and 26-9 respectively.

The final match of the tour, the Fourth Test against South Africa, was played in Johannesburg on 27 July. The Springboks were desperate to salvage something from the tour and avoid a 4-0 whitewash. Fly-half Jackie Snyman gave them the lead with a penalty kick after five minutes but the Lions responded with a try from the forward Roger Uttley, converted by Phil Bennett. Another penalty from Snyman brought the scores level but Andy Irvine's try put the Lions in the lead 10-6 at half-time. In the second half

Peter Cronje went over for a try that again levelled the score. A third penalty from Snyman put the Springboks in the lead but this was matched by one from Irvine. With the score 13-13, and the Lions pressing for a winning try, the Irish flanker Fergus Slattery burst through the desperate South African defence and appeared to have scored. Even the Springboks assumed he had. The referee, however, decided he hadn't grounded the ball properly. As the Lions continued their attack, with four minutes still to go, he also decided to blow his whistle to bring the game to a premature end.

The referee, who was South African, is reputed to have told some Lions players who approached, and reproached, him after the game, 'Look, boys, I have to live here'.

June

The biggest explosion in Britain in peacetime destroys a chemical plant in Lincolnshire. A bomb goes off in the Houses of Parliament. A supposedly revolutionary first aid technique is announced and a new era in retailing dawns. Public nudity is all the rage as 'streaking' becomes a popular pastime. Confrontations between police and demonstrators in London end in the death of young student. A Soviet ballet dancer defects to the West. Martin Luther King's mother is shot dead in a church in Atlanta, Georgia.

Flixborough Disaster

Just before 5pm on Saturday 1 June, there was a colossal explosion at the Nypro (UK) chemical plant near the village of Flixborough in Lincolnshire. Twenty-eight people were killed, eighteen of them in the plant's control room when the windows blew in and the roof collapsed on top of them. Many others were injured. In all likelihood, the casualties would have been significantly worse had the accident happened on a weekday, when most of the workforce would have been on site, rather than on a Saturday when only an unlucky few were present. At the time it was the biggest explosion in Britain during peacetime, surpassed only 31 years later by that at the Buncefield oil depot in Hertfordshire. Property in Flixborough itself and other neighbouring villages was damaged, and the sound it made could be heard in Grimsby, more than 30 miles away. The resulting fires continued to burn for more than a week after the original explosion.

The Flixborough plant produced caprolactam, a chemical involved in the manufacture of nylon. Several weeks before the explosion, a crack was found in one of the reactors on the site and a pipe was installed so that the area of the potential leak could be bypassed and production continue. During the afternoon of 1 June, this temporary pipe ruptured and large quantities of a highly flammable substance called cyclohexane were released. This, it is thought, ignited and caused the catastrophic explosion. One of the workers who was on site but survived later described his experience. 'I felt the blast from a terrific explosion which had occurred somewhere behind me,' he said. 'The blast was such that it threw me full length across the road. Debris then began to fall all around me and I was covered with oil which fell out of the sky.'

A reporter from the *Hull Daily Mail* who was present on the day later recalled what he had seen in the village of Flixborough itself at 5am on the day after the disaster. 'House after house was devastated, roofs torn away, bricks and tiles flung on to gardens... Half-eaten meals covered in shattered glass lay on tables, deck chairs were scattered on patios, children's bicycles lay abandoned by the roadside. Above it all, the mile-high plume of smoke still rose as fires continued to burn amid the twisted wreckage of what had been the Nypro plant.'

An inquiry, chaired by a QC, sat for 70 days between September 1974 and February 1975 to examine the causes of the disaster and to identify any lessons that could be learned from it. Taking evidence from more than 150 witnesses, the inquiry drew attention to failings surrounding the installation of the bypass pipe and to an array of other factors which had combined to create the circumstances in which the tragedy could occur. Debate still continues to this day about the exact nature of events leading to the explosion but its one positive outcome was an increased awareness that the safety regulations surrounding industrial processes such as those that took place at Flixborough needed to be made much more rigorous.

Explosion in the Houses of Parliament

Just before 8.30 on the morning of 17 June, a bomb exploded in a corner of Westminster Hall, the oldest part of the Palace of Westminster still in existence, dating back to 1097 and the reign of William II. A warning had been telephoned to the Press Association, giving a codeword known to be used by the IRA but it had been received only six minutes before the bomb went off. The politician David Steel, then Liberal Chief Whip, was close to the building at the time. 'I looked through Westminster Hall and the whole hall was filled with dust,' he told the BBC. 'A few minutes later it was possible to see flames shooting up through the windows.' The bomb had damaged and then ignited a gas main. Firemen fought to bring the resulting blaze under control throughout the morning. Eleven people were injured and an annex containing offices was destroyed. Thankfully, none of the injuries was life-threatening and the great hall itself suffered only superficial damage. The spectacular hammerbeam roof, built in the reign of Richard II, survived intact. However, as a writer in the *Times* noted, the bombing hit at the heart of the British establishment and 'there could be few more dramatic ways of symbolising defiance of the spirit of orderly government represented by parliament'. The bombing revealed what now seems the remarkably lax security on the parliamentary estate. As the Labour MP Tam Dalyell later admitted, 'No one expected in those days that the House of Commons would be a target'.

The following month saw an attack on another obvious symbol of British power when a bomb containing 10 pounds of explosives went off at the Tower of London. This time no warning was given. It had been planted in the armoury of the White Tower, positioned next to the wooden carriage of an eighteenth-century bronze cannon which was hurled into the air. Around fifty visitors, many of them German and Scandinavian tourists, were in the room at the time. One man who was standing just outside the White Tower heard 'a tremendous explosion and then nothing and then a lot of children screaming'. The head of Scotland Yard's Bomb Squad reported that 'it was an indiscriminate attack', and was 'designed to create as much trouble and injury as possible'. The explosion killed Dorothy Household, a librarian from Lewisham, and injured dozens of others, including children. Some lost limbs and a child's foot was found beneath the bronze cannon. Although no one claimed responsibility for the bombing, it has always been assumed that it was another bloody episode in the Provisional IRA's campaign on mainland Britain.

Heimlich Manouevre First Described

An article published in the 1 June issue of the magazine *Emergency Medicine* introduced a new term into the vocabulary of emergency first aid. It was written by the American surgeon Henry Heimlich and it had the eye-catching title 'Pop Goes the Café Coronary'. The 'café coronary' was an informal term applied to an incident when an individual, usually in a café or restaurant or at the dinner table, begins to choke, turns blue in the face and, in the worst cases, dies within minutes. To an onlooker, the person might seem to be suffering from a heart attack. In reality, food has been caught in the windpipe and they cannot breathe.

According to Heimlich in his 1974 article, nearly 4,000 people died this way every year in the USA. However, help was at hand because he, Henry Heimlich, had devised a brilliant method of dislodging any food thus caught. All anybody needed to do if faced by someone choking in this way was to stand behind the sufferer and wrap both arms around them 'just below the belt line'. Then, in Heimlich's own words, 'the rescuer rapidly and strongly presses into the victim's abdomen, forcing the diaphragm upwards, compressing the lungs, and expelling the obstructing bolus'. This was what came to be popularly known as the 'Heimlich Manouevre'. Alarmingly, Heimlich's initial experiments to test his theory had been carried out on four beagles rather than human beings. (The ethical difficulties of performing the tests on the latter are obvious, although, had they any choice in the matter, the beagles might also have objected to repeated chokings inflicted on them in the name of medical science.)

The manouevre was controversial from the beginning and many doctors refused to acknowledge any merit in it. Indeed, some argued that, in comparison with previously tried and tested methods, such as simply vigorously slapping the sufferer's back in order to dislodge the choking foodstuff, it might prove positively dangerous. However, Heimlich proved a brilliant cheerleader for his ideas, appearing on TV talk shows to demonstrate them and losing no opportunity to sing their praises. He soon became a minor celebrity and the Heimlich Manouevre made headlines both in America and around the world.

Many people were persuaded by his advocacy but many remained deeply sceptical of his claims. 'There was never any science here,' one of his critics argued. 'Heimlich overpowered science all along the way with his slick tactics and intimidation, and everyone... caved in.' Even one of Heimlich's own sons, Peter, became a fierce critic. Permanently estranged from his father, he called him 'a spectacular con man and serial liar' and stated bluntly that 'the only thing my father ever invented was his own mythology'. More than 40 years after his controversial article, aged 96 and living in a Cincinnati care home, Heimlich reported that he had saved the life of a fellow resident by using his technique to stop her choking on a hamburger. Doubt has been cast on the truth of this, as on so many of Heimlich's claims.

Barcode in Shopping

In a branch of Marsh Supermarkets in Troy, Ohio, an event took place on 26 June which heralded a new era in shopping. At one minute past 8am, a customer approached a checkout with a trolley. The checkout woman, Sharon Buchanan, was given a 10-pack of Wrigley's Juicy Fruit chewing gum and scanned it. The cash register rang up 67 cents. This was the first use of a barcode in retailing history. In most ways, it was a staged event. The 'customer' was Clyde Dawson, who was head of research and development for the supermarket chain, and he had deliberately picked out the gum for a reason. Critics of barcode technology had been claiming that it was impossible to print one on something as small as a pack of chewing gum. Dawson, Wrigleys and all advocates of the future of barcoding were keen to prove them wrong.

Sharon Buchanan had turned up for work that morning, not knowing that she was about to participate in a moment of retail history. She did notice that there were more people gathered around the tills than she expected to see. These, she discovered, were engineers who had been busy overnight installing a barcode scanner on her checkout and testing that it worked. Sharon was given a very brief training session before Clyde Dawson approached with his trolley and his Juicy Fruit gum. It was all over in a matter of minutes but she had a story she could retell for the rest of her life. 'It was my 15 minutes of fame,' she later said.

The barcode had been invented decades earlier by a man named Joseph Woodland who had tested his first ideas by drawing them in the sand on a Florida beach. He gained a patent for his invention in 1952 but was unable to find any means of making it commercially viable. He sold it for what amounted to a pittance of $15,000. Attempts to refine and improve the technology so that it could be used in retail continued for decades without success. Giant companies like RCA, which had bought Woodland's patent, and IBM, which now employed Woodland himself, competed for the holy grail of an easily readable barcode. It was not until the development of the UPC or Universal Product Code that the latter made the breakthrough that led to the historic purchase in Marsh Supermarket in Troy, Ohio. Clyde Dawson passed away in 2014; Sharon

Buchanan in 2017; the packet of Juicy Fruit gum that provided both of them with their brief moment in history's spotlight is now in the collection of the National Museum of American History, part of the Smithsonian Institution. Barcodes themselves are everywhere.

Ray Stevens' 'The Streak' Reaches Number One in the UK Singles Chart

A novelty comedy song by the country singer Ray Stevens reached the top spot in the UK Singles chart on 11 June, staying there for one week only. It was entitled 'The Streak' and was inspired by the recent vogue for streaking – running naked – in public places. The lyrics described the activities of one such exhibitionist:

> 'Oh yes, they call him the Streak
> He likes to show off his physique
> If there's an audience to be found
> He'll be streakin' around
> Invitin' public critique.'

During the song, a news reporter is heard commenting on the Streak's performances and eliciting the opinion of a bystander who is most concerned that his wife should not be shocked by them ('Don't look, Ethel.') To no listener's great surprise, Ethel not only looks but, towards the end of the song, strips off herself and joins the Streak.

Of course, public nudity had been recorded in the past. As far back as 1667, Pepys had described a man who strode naked through Westminster Hall, 'only very civilly tied about the privates to avoid scandal'. The man was a Quaker named Solomon Eagle and his impulse to strip off was religious in origin. The streakers of the 1970s were mostly motivated by a sense of fun, drink, the need to win a bet or a longing for their 15 minutes of fame. The term 'streaking' had been used in the 1960s and university students in America took it up in 1973. In March of the following year, more than fifteen hundred students at the University of Georgia chose to streak en masse across their campus in the town of Athens. The following month a streaker appeared, nude and giving the two-fingered peace sign, at the Oscars ceremony just as David Niven was about to present the award for Best Picture in front of a live TV audience. Niven was far too urbane an individual to be put off his stride by a naked man galloping across the stage. 'Isn't it fascinating to think,' he remarked, 'that probably the only laugh that man will ever get in his life is by stripping off his clothes and showing his shortcomings?'

1974 was also the year in which streaking became a recognisable craze in the UK. Some of the most tempting arenas in which streakers could operate were sporting ones. Football's first streaker was probably John Taylor, a 44-year-old gentleman from Newbury, who was dared by his mates to divest himself of his clothing and run on to the pitch at the Arsenal v. Manchester City match of 23 March. He did so and ran around the Highbury ground until apprehended by three policemen. One cannot be sure but drink may have been taken. On the following Monday, Mr Taylor appeared before a magistrate and was fined £10 for 'using insulting behaviour whereby a breach of the peace was likely to be occasioned'.

On 20 April an Australian named Michael O'Brien was attending a rugby match at Twickenham between England and France when he accepted a drunken bet from his friends that he would not strip naked and race across the pitch from one touchline to the other. Nude as nature intended, he set off but was pursued and captured by two policemen. One of the officers, PC Bruce Perry, gallantly shielded O'Brien's manhood from continued public exposure with his policeman's helmet and, with the crowd's cheers ringing in their ears, the pair became the subject of a famous photograph, regularly reproduced in the years since the streak. 'It was a cold day,' Perry later reported (less gallantly), 'and he didn't have anything to be proud of.' O'Brien later became a successful stockbroker back in Australia.

Red Lion Square Disorder

At the beginning of the month, the far-right, neo-fascist National Front (NF) announced a march through central London which would be held on 15 June. It would make its way to Conway Hall in Red Lion Square where there would be a talk on the subject of stopping immigration and starting repatriation. Plans were immediately made to mount a counter-demonstration. Initially, the prime movers were members of Liberation, an anti-colonial organisation which had been in existence since the 1950s. However, on the day, it would include not only several far-left groups, from the Workers' Revolutionary Party to the International Marxist Group (IMG), but also the National Union of Students. The IMG were determined to deny the National Front access to Conway Hall and formed picket lines in front of the main entrance. The police, some of them mounted, struggled to keep the left-wing protesters apart from close to a thousand NF marchers. Violent clashes between the various groups ensued and it was during these that the day's major tragedy occurred.

Kevin Gately was a maths student at the University of Warwick. He had never been on a political demonstration before and he would not get the opportunity to go on one again.

Exceptionally tall – at least 6 feet 7 inches – and red-haired, Gately was not an easy man to lose in a crowd. He can be identified in press photos of the day because he is towering above others in the demonstration. At some point during the chaos that was engulfing Red Lion Square, and in some way that has never been conclusively explained, Kevin Gately was hit on the head. A *Guardian* reporter at the scene wrote that, 'he was left prone and motionless on the ground as the police drove demonstrators back. We saw his body emerge, rather as a rugby ball comes slowly out of a scrum, as the police cordon gradually moved forward.' Lying unconscious on the ground 'amid a litter of broken placards, torn banners and lost shoes', Gately was picked up by police officers and carried first to a St John Ambulance post and then to University College Hospital. There he died, the first person to have lost their life during a demonstration in Britain since 1919.

The inquest into his death took place at the beginning of July. Giving evidence, one witness reported that Gately's eyes were closed at the time he collapsed. 'I assumed that he had fainted. He was totally unconscious before he hit the ground. He fell sideways as his knees buckled.' The inquest jury delivered a verdict of misadventure but this did not satisfy those who were convinced that the police or right-wing demonstrators were involved in the young man's death. 'When you get police diving in with truncheons and horses and somebody is killed in circumstances like this,' one of the organisers from Liberation was quoted as saying, 'I would call it murder.' A public inquiry, chaired by Lord Scarman (later chair of the inquiry into the 1981 Brixton riots), was convened in September to look into the events of 15 June. Its report was published the following year. Its verdict on Kevin Gately's death was little different to that of the inquest. 'There is no evidence that he was struck any blow by any policeman or injured in any way by a police horse: it is not even possible to say whether it was a blow, a fall, a kick or being trampled on which caused the superficially tiny injury that led to his brain haemorrhage.'

Mikhail Baryshnikov Defects

The Soviet Union faced a dilemma in the 1960s and 1970s. The regime wanted its musicians and artistes to visit the West in order to demonstrate the sophistication and strength of Soviet culture. Unfortunately, when they toured the West, many musicians and artistes decided they didn't want to go back home. High-profile defections like those of the ballet dancers Rudolf Nureyev and Natalia Makarova cast the Soviet Union in a poor light. The KGB worked hard to keep touring performers under constant surveillance but this was not always successful. Another significant defection took place in June 1974.

Mikhail Baryshnikov was born in Riga, which was then the capital of the Latvian Soviet Socialist Republic and part of the USSR, in 1948. After beginning his dance studies in his home city at the age of 12, he later moved to Leningrad's Vaganova Academy, one of the most prestigious schools of classical ballet, and was soon picking up prizes for his dancing. He joined the Kirov Ballet (now the Mariinsky) in 1967 and immediately began to make his mark in leading roles. The critic Clive Barnes called the young Baryshnikov, when he was still performing in the Soviet Union, 'the most perfect dancer I have ever seen'.

In June 1974, Baryshnikov was touring Canada with the most famous of all Russian ballet companies, the Bolshoi. On the 29th of the month, in Toronto, he escaped the vigilance of his KGB minder after a performance, ran to a waiting car, and was whisked away into hiding. Just over a decade later, he described his escape: 'I was running, the getaway car was waiting a few blocks away as we were boarding on the group's bus. KGB was watching us. It was actually funny. Fans are waiting for me outside the stage door, and I walk out and I start to run, and they start to run after me for autograph. They were laughing, I was running for my life.' His request for political asylum in Canada was granted and he was able to emerge from hiding to take up his career again, but this time in the West.

Baryshnikov has always maintained that his decision to defect was as much an artistic as a political one. 'When I was in Toronto,' he told a journalist in his first post-defection interview, 'I finally decided that if I let the opportunity of expanding my art in the West slip by, it would haunt me always... I want to work with some of the West's great choreographers if they think I am worthy of their creations.' In the years since his defection he has been able to do so. He has danced with the American Ballet Theatre and worked with them on fresh versions of classics such as *The Nutcracker*; he has collaborated with the legendary choreographer George Balanchine; he has established his own company, the White Oak Dance Project; and, in 2005, founded the Baryshnikov Arts Center in New York. In addition, he became something of a Hollywood star, appearing with the American tap dancer Gregory Hines in *White Nights* and opposite Gene Hackman in the 1991 action thriller *Company Business*.

Assassination of Martin Luther King's Mother

Many people know that the American civil rights activist Martin Luther King Jr was assassinated in 1968; far fewer are aware that his mother suffered the same fate six years later. On 30 June, Alberta King was sitting at the organ of the Ebenezer Baptist Church in Atlanta, Georgia, where she was director of the choir, when a young man in his early twenties named Marcus Wayne Chenault shot her twice. She was rushed to the nearest hospital but died soon after her arrival there.

Chenault, who told police that 'all Christians are my enemies', was an adherent of a new religious group known as the Black Hebrew Israelites who believed that African-Americans were descendants of the ancient Israelites. Many of them considered black church leaders to be liars who were deceiving and defrauding their congregations. Chenault's original intention had been to kill the Reverend Jesse Jackson in Chicago but he had decided against this and instead travelled south to Georgia. Inside the Ebenezer Baptist Church he hoped to assassinate Martin Luther King Sr but the pastor was elsewhere that Sunday. When Chenault could not see his original target, he stood up, shouting, 'You are serving a false God!', and fired at Alberta King who was playing the organ. He also turned his weapon on the rest of the congregation, shooting wildly, killing one of the church deacons, Edward Boykin, and wounding another worshipper, a retired teacher named Jimmie Mitchell. As he attempted to reload his pistol, Chenault was subdued by several men from the church choir. One of them later told journalists, 'He was delirious. He appeared to be in a fever. He said over and over, "The war did this to me. It's the war."' Chenault was a Vietnam veteran and had suffered from mental illness since his return home.

In the wake of the shooting, the congregation and others gathered outside the Ebenezer Baptist Church. 'There were people everywhere,' Alberta King's daughter, Christine, remembered. 'There was a throng of onlookers. When I looked in their eyes I saw what is often described as "the thousand-yard stare". It was a kind of blankness I'd never seen before. They were bewildered and in shock.

Many were crying; most had their hands pressed to their mouths in disbelief.' Martin Luther King Jr's mother had been shot and fatally wounded only a hundred yards away from where her famous son lay buried.

Convicted of first-degree murder, Chenault faced execution but, partly because of the King family's expressed opposition to the death penalty, his sentence was changed to life imprisonment. He died of a stroke in 1995, aged 44.

July

In Argentina President Juan Peron dies and is replaced
by his wife Isabel. Hosts West Germany meet favourites
the Netherlands in the World Cup Final. Turkey invades
Cyprus. American news presenter Christine Chubbuck
commits suicide live on TV. The Warsaw Radio Mast,
then the world's tallest structure, comes into service. In
Huntsville, Texas, three prison inmates hold 15 people
hostage in an eleven-day stand-off with the authorities.
At Wimbledon, the Americans Jimmy Connors and
Chris Evert triumph.

Death of Juan Peron

In early 1973, the exiled Argentine general and politician, Juan Peron, was contemplating the possibilities of a comeback. He had first served as his country's president 27 years earlier when his First Lady had been his second wife, Eva, better known as Evita, fated to be the future subject of an Andrew Lloyd Webber musical. The couple had been immensely popular with swathes of Argentine's working classes because of the government's commitment to improving the lot of the poor but Peron had also presided over an authoritarian regime in which political opponents were imprisoned and tortured, and refuge was given to ex-Nazis such as Josef Mengele and Adolf Eichmann. He was nonetheless re-elected for a second term in 1952 but Evita died of cancer, aged only 33, in that same year. She had been a major reason for her husband's popularity and, without her at his side, he began to lose support.

The public's increasing dissatisfaction with their president, largely brought about by his inability to deal with the economic difficulties the country faced, was compounded by his relationship with Nelly Rivas, a young girl who was only 14 years old at the time she found a place in the 59-year-old president's heart and, it was strongly rumoured, his bed. In 1955, Peron was overthrown in a military coup and driven into exile, forced to spend many years abroad, mostly in Spain.

During all these years of exile, he continued to influence the politics of his home country and the Peronist movement still had millions of supporters. In March 1973, a general election was held within Argentina, and, although

Peron himself was barred from standing in it, one of his leading allies, Hector Campora, was chosen as president. He took office in May and Peron returned to the country the following month to be greeted by enormous crowds at the airport. Some estimates suggest that more than 3 million people were gathered to welcome him, although the occasion ended in bloodshed when right-wing Peronist snipers opened fire on other Peronists from the left wing of his supporters.

Campora and his vice-president resigned in July, opening a path to new elections in which Peron could now participate. He won 62 per cent of the vote and began his third term as president in October. By this time, he was in his late seventies and his health was poor. He was suffering from an enlarged prostate and from heart disease. It was later suggested that his mental powers were flagging and even that he was in the first stages of dementia. Following a series of heart attacks and a sequence of bulletins from his doctors, each announcing a new deterioration in his health, Peron died in the early afternoon of 1 July 1974. He was succeeded as president by his third wife, Maria Estela, better known as Isabel, who had dashed back from Europe, where she had been participating in a trade mission, on first hearing of his illness. A former cabaret dancer, she became, at the age of 43, the youngest South American head of state at the time.

Her first concern was to avoid the turmoil that could so often accompany transitions of power in South America and she appealed to 'friends and opponents alike to put aside their personal passions' after the death of her husband whom she called 'this great apostle of peace and non-violence', a description that might have surprised some of those who had opposed him in the past. One of the oddest commemorations of Peron's passing took place not in Argentina but across the Atlantic in West Germany where the World Cup was taking place (see below). On 3 July, two days after the general's death, four matches kicked off at various times in the day. One of them was Argentina v. East Germany where a minute's silence before the game might have been understandable. Instead FIFA decreed, for now unfathomable reasons, that there would be thirty seconds of silence in the middle of all four matches. Ten minutes into each game, proceedings halted at the referee's whistle and players from countries such as Holland, Poland and Yugoslavia had to stand still to reflect on the death of an elderly politician many thousands of miles away.

World Cup Final

The 1974 World Cup was held in West Germany and the final was played on 7 July in Munich's Olympiastadion which had been the main venue for the 1972 Olympic Games. The tournament had begun just over three weeks earlier with a match at the Waldstadion, Frankfurt between the holders Brazil and Yugoslavia. Despite the attacking talent on display (the Brazil team included Jairzinho who had been their top scorer in the previous World Cup), it ended in a 0-0 draw.

In the first round of matches, West Germany and East Germany were both in Group 1. East Germany topped the group, beating their neighbours 1-0 in a needle match at

Hamburg but the West Germans went through to the next round in second place. Yugoslavia headed Group 2, largely because of their 9-0 victory over Zaire, and Scotland, the only British team in the competition, were unlucky to exit after drawing with both Brazil and the Yugoslavs but failing to score more than two goals against the African side. Group 3 went to the Netherlands, captained by the late Johan Cruyff, three times winner of the Ballon d'Or as European Footballer of the Year, and generally considered one of the greatest players of the twentieth century. Unsurprisingly, Holland were among the favourites to reach the final. Sweden achieved second place. (It was in the Group 3 match between the Netherlands and Sweden that one of the defining moments of the 1974 World Cup occurred when Cruyff sold the Swedish right-back Jan Olsson 'the mother of all dummies' in what has since come to be known as the 'Cruyff Turn'.) Poland, the only team to gain maximum points in the first round, went through from Group 4 with Argentina whose goal difference was marginally better than Italy's.

Eight teams, the winners and runners-up in each group, now went forward to the second round. Unlike the competition today, the World Cup in 1974 had no knockout round at this stage. Instead the eight teams were organised into two groups of four. The winners of each group would progress to the final; the runners-up to the third place play-off. In Group A, the Dutch comfortably beat East Germany and Argentina, the latter by four goals to nil. The deciding match was between them and Brazil who had also won their games against the other two teams in the group. It proved a disappointing contest in which the South Americans chose aggressive tactics to unsettle their opponents. One of their defenders, Luis Pereira, was eventually sent off in the 84th minute but, by that time, the Dutch had scored two goals through Cruyff and Neeskens and had the game in the bag. In Group B the competition for a place in the final was between West Germany and Poland who had both won their matches against Yugoslavia and Sweden, the other teams in the group. In the deciding match West Germany won 1-0, the only goal of the game scored by their talismanic striker, Gerd Müller.

On 6 July Poland and Brazil played for third place, the East Europeans winning by a single goal scored by winger Grzegorz Lato. So onto the final on the following day between host nation West Germany and the much-fancied favourites, Holland. It was scheduled to kick off at 4pm but the start was delayed when it was realised that there were no corner flags. The closing ceremony for the tournament had taken place immediately before the final and the flags had been removed for that. Nobody had remembered to put them back. Jack Taylor, the English referee, who had charge of the match, took responsibility for replacing them. 'When you come to a World Cup final in Germany, such an efficient nation who never make mistakes, and there's no corner flags you can't believe it,' he recalled. 'There's millions of people watching and here I am, this one little guy, coming all the way around the pitch sticking corner flags in.' Once the task had been completed, the match could begin.

The Dutch, led by Cruyff, had played some entrancing football in their earlier games and were clear favourites. They scored within two minutes, after Cruyff, embarking on a solo run, was brought down in the penalty area before a German player had even touched the ball. Jack Taylor pointed to the spot and Johann Neeskens put the ball past the German goalkeeper, Sepp Maier. For a while it looked as if the match might be one-sided and the Netherlands emerge as easy winners but the Germans, under Franz Beckenbauer's captaincy, clung on without conceding another goal. In the 25th minute, they were awarded their own penalty when Bernd Hölzenbein was fouled in the box. Left-back Paul Breitner put the ball in the net. Encouraged by this, the Germans grew in confidence and they scored again just before half-time when Gerd Müller, playing his final match in an international career which brought him an astonishing 68 goals in 62 appearances, beat the Dutch goalkeeper Jongbloed. After the interval, the Dutch threw everything at their opponents but the Germans remained resolute in defence and Cruyff and his men could not find an equaliser. When Taylor blew his whistle for the end of the contest, the score was still 2-1. Beckenbauer's West Germans had triumphed; the Dutch, one of the finest and most innovative international sides of all time, had lost a game most neutral observers had expected them to win.

Coup and Invasion in Cyprus

The history of Cyprus in the post-war years was constantly bedevilled by the question of *enosis* or union with Greece. The most powerful figure in Cypriot politics for many years was Archbishop Makarios, head of the country's Orthodox Church, who had been identified with *enosis* during the years that Cyprus was under British rule but moved away from any commitment to it after independence and his own election as president. His emphasis was now more on the integration of the Greek and Turkish communities on the island rather than on solely Greek interests.

In 1973, Makarios had been returned for a third term as the head of state but opposition to him was growing. Heading this was EOKA-B, a group which aimed to bring about *enosis*, by violent means if necessary. After a number of terrorist attacks in Cyprus, Makarios declared EOKA-B an illegal organisation but it continued to have the support of the military junta which then ruled Greece. A coup against the Archbishop's government was in the making.

Early on the morning of 15 July, tanks began to shell the presidential palace in Nicosia. Makarios was initially reported to have met his death during the coup. However, although the palace was eventually burnt to the ground, he had escaped through a rear entrance soon after the shelling began and had succeeded in making his way to the coastal city of Paphos. From there he had been taken by plane to Malta and on to London where he had a meeting with Harold Wilson and Jim Callaghan, then Foreign Secretary, who assured him that Britain would recognise no one else as lawful president of his country. According to Wilson, he also arranged with an Orthodox church in London for the archbishop to be supplied with a clean cassock. Freshly cassocked, Makarios flew to New York to address the UN Security Council and argue his case that the Greek junta was responsible for the coup.

Back in Cyprus, Makarios had been replaced by a former journalist and fervent advocate of *enosis*, Nikos

Sampson, who managed a mere eight days as president before resigning. Even in such a short period of power, Sampson succeeded in instituting a mini-reign of terror against both Makarios supporters and left-wing opponents of his rule and hundreds lost their lives. In response to the Greek-backed coup, which represented a severe threat to the Turkish citizens of Cyprus, Turkish forces had been immediately put on high alert. The Turkish prime minister, Bülent Ecevit, followed Makarios's example and travelled to London but no way through the crisis could be found. The Turkish government expressed unwillingness to negotiate with the Greeks and the Greek junta showed no interest in meeting with the Turks. On 19 July, Ecevit phoned his commander-in-chief from London and authorised him to go ahead with plans to invade Cyprus. On the following day, Turkish troops landed west of the port of Kyrenia and paratroopers dropped from the skies on to Cypriot soil. Within days a ceasefire had been brokered by the UN but the area around Nicosia in particular had already seen some heavy fighting and many deaths.

Events continued to move swiftly in both Greece and Cyprus. On 23-24 July, the Greek junta collapsed and Constantine Karamanlis, who had been prime minister in the 1960s before the military took control, ended his exile in Paris and returned to power. In Cyprus, Sampson stepped down and was replaced as president by Glafcos Clerides. A conference in Geneva was called at the end of July with representatives from both sides in Cyprus and the foreign ministers of Britain, Greece and Turkey. However, Turkey, which, following the change of government in Greece, had been prepared to accept the UN call for a ceasefire, continued to send troops into Cyprus and refused point blank to consider any agreement that involved the withdrawal of their military forces from the island. As the politicians wrangled, events on the ground changed. In the middle of August, the Turkish army broke out of their lines and pushed further south, bringing close to 40 per cent of the island under its control. Ecevit agreed to a ceasefire on 16 August but, by that time, the damage had been done. The island was effectively partitioned. It has remained so ever since.

American Victories at Wimbledon

Both the men's and the women's singles finals at Wimbledon in 1974 were won by young American players. Not only that, the two victors, Chris Evert and Jimmy Connors, to the delight of tabloid newspapers around the world, were dating one another. On 5 July, Evert beat Olga Morozova from the Soviet Union who had defeated the defending champion Billie Jean King in the quarter-finals and the great British hope, Virginia Wade, in the semis. In the final she was blown away by Evert who had had an easier passage via wins against Helga Masthoff and Kerry Melville. It took the American no more than an hour to triumph. She won the first set 6-0 and, although her Russian opponent rallied a little in the second, the result was never in doubt. Evert took the second set 6-4. At 19, she was the youngest winner since Maureen 'Little Mo' Connolly took the title in 1952, aged 17. 'I know I'll be playing at Wimbledon for years to come,' she said after her victory. 'But I was thinking a few years ahead when Billie Jean (King) and Margaret (Court) might retire. I never expected to win Wimbledon this year.'

The men's final, played on the following day, also exemplified the passing of an older generation and the arrival of a new. Jimmy Connors was 21 years old, and in the middle of a dream year that eventually brought him 15 victories in the 21 tournaments he entered, including three Grand Slams. His opponent, Ken Rosewall, was an Australian veteran who had first played at Wimbledon in 1952 and was now 39 years old. He had enjoyed a wonderful career and this was his final chance to win the one Grand Slam title that had eluded him. Most of the neutrals in the crowd were on his side but it was all to no avail. Connors swept to victory in straight sets, winning 6-1, 6-1, 6-4. Many tennis fans lamented what they saw as the end of an era. As *The Observer*'s Jon Henderson put it many years later, 'There was a palpable sense of nostalgia as tennis stood on the edge of a paradigm shift. Rosewall was a brilliant representative of the fading age of elegance, a player for whom tennis was about touch, placement and exquisite variations.' By contrast, Connors seemed like 'a young American punk'. His was a game that depended on power not elegance and the future belonged to him.

Warsaw Radio Mast Begins Transmissions

The skyscraper known as the Burj Khalifa in Dubai has been far and away the world's tallest structure since it was completed in 2010. The Merdeka Tower, a 118-storey office and residential block in Kuala Lumpur, opened in 2022, now takes second place. The third tallest structure ever built was finished in 1974. It was a radio mast in a tiny village named Konstantynów, some 50 miles west of the Polish capital, Warsaw, and it entered regular service on 22 July which was celebrated from 1944 to 1989 as the 'National Day of the Rebirth of Poland'. Designed by an engineer named Jan Polak, it was 646 metres tall or 2,121 feet. For seventeen years it acted as a transmitter for Warsaw Radio-Television. Its signal could be picked up throughout Europe, in many parts of Africa and across the Atlantic in the USA. It has even been claimed that it could be picked up by radios in polar stations in Antarctica.

The radio mast's reign as the world's tallest structure did not last long. After only a decade it was showing distinct signs of wear and tear. Gusts of wind had caused minor structural damage but much worse was to come. In 1991, during the replacement of some frayed guy wires, one of the main supporting cables needed to be temporarily disconnected. In the course of doing this, while the main cable was loosened and the temporary ones had yet to be fully connected, a sudden, strong gust of wind twisted the mast tower. Now unsupported, the mast bent and snapped about halfway up its 646 metres and the entire structure collapsed. No one was injured but two employees of the construction company responsible for maintaining the mast were sent to jail. Rebuilding it was mooted but was met with fierce opposition by locals who doubted its safety in the future and had no desire to witness large chunks of metal crashing into their homes.

The plans for reconstruction were abandoned. Parts of the mast's wreckage can still be seen at the site.

Shocking Event on Live TV

Journalists are well advised not to become news stories themselves. One who did so in the most dramatic and tragic of circumstances was 29-year-old Christine Chubbuck, a reporter and presenter for the Florida TV station WXLT. Born in Ohio, where she grew up, Chubbuck took a degree in broadcasting from Boston University and went on to a series of jobs with small radio and TV companies. She joined her last employer in 1973 and by the August of that year she was hosting *Suncoast Digest*, a morning talk show on the station in which she interviewed local people.

The morning of 15 July began like any other, although some of her co-workers later suggested that she was markedly more cheerful than she ordinarily was. She surprised them by saying that she would open the show with a segment of news before moving on to her scheduled interview. This was not her normal practice but she proceeded to cover three national stories over the next eight minutes. In the midst of reading a fourth story, there was a technical hitch with the film that was intended to accompany it. It failed to roll. Chubbuck paused, turned to the camera and announced, 'in keeping with the WXLT practice of presenting the most immediate and complete reports of local blood and guts news, TV 40 presents what is believed to be a television first. In living colour, an exclusive coverage of an attempted suicide.' She then drew a gun from her bag and shot herself behind her right ear. The programme director swiftly shut down the broadcast and the station was soon showing a movie. Chubbuck was rushed to the nearest hospital where she died some fourteen hours after her very public act of despair.

She had suffered from depression for years (she had survived a drugs overdose in 1970) and her family knew about her struggles with her mental health. They had not informed anyone at WXLT because they feared this might jeopardise her job prospects. A week before the 15th, she herself had spoken to the channel's night editor of killing herself on air but he had assumed this was merely an example of her 'sick' sense of humour and made no response. Her body was cremated and her ashes scattered in the Gulf of Mexico. The minister at her funeral service expressed the sense of shock and bewilderment so many of those who knew her felt when he said, 'We suffer at our sense of loss, we are frightened by her rage, we are guilty in the face of her rejection, we are hurt by her choice of isolation and we are confused by her message'. The recording of Chubbuck's suicide reportedly still exists, although it has not been seen since the day of her death. Faked footage purporting to show her shooting herself has surfaced on YouTube but the real footage is said to be locked away in the safe of a major law firm. A feature film based on her life and death, *Christine*, was released in 2016 starring Rebecca Hall in the title role.

Huntsville Prison Siege

What was one of the longest sieges involving the taking of hostages in American history began in the state penitentiary in Huntsville, Texas in July 1974 and lasted into the following month. The ruthless Mexican-American drug lord Federico Gomez Carrasco, serving a life sentence after his capture in a shootout with police at a San Antonio motel, was the ringleader of a small gang of prisoners making a desperate bid for freedom. Through his outside connections, he had succeeded in having pistols and ammunition smuggled into the prison kitchens where he was able to get his hands on them. The guns had arrived in a hollowed-out ham, the ammunition in a giant tin of peaches. On the afternoon of 24 July, together with two associates, Rodolpho Dominguez and Ignacio Cuevas, Carrasco entered the prison library, firing off several shots and rounding up all the people there. Initially these numbered about 80 but he realised that he could not hope to keep control of so many and he began to release them in batches of five from the now barricaded library. He was left with 15 hostages – 4 fellow inmates and 11 prison workers. Thus began an 11-day stand-off in which Carrasco attempted to engineer his escape and the authorities struggled to end the crisis without bloodshed.

Negotiations began with the prison's warden, HH Husbands, and with the director of the Texas Department of Corrections, WJ Estelle. As word spread of what was taking place in Huntsville, FBI agents arrived to assist the local authorities and the media came to the town en masse. Carrasco and his sidekicks made a series of demands – for smart clothing, walkie talkies and protective helmets – and most of these were met. However, Husbands and Estelle were determined not to allow the three prisoners to escape and so the siege dragged on. One of the hostages was released after what appeared to be a heart attack; another decided that this was a good tactic to employ to gain his own freedom and faked a similar illness. He too was released. A third hostage, fearing that he had angered Carrasco and that his life was in danger, successfully escaped the library. Many of the remaining hostages were deeply religious and kept up their spirits by singing hymns such as 'Amazing Grace' and 'Oh, How I Love Jesus'. Carrasco was a volatile man. He could be polite and almost charming one minute, ferociously aggressive the next. 'I believe Carrasco made an attempt to be shown as a gentleman criminal,' one of the hostages later reported. 'He treated us with a great deal of respect and kindness – except, of course, when he'd tell us, "I'm going to shoot you in 20 minutes". And he did that three or four times a day.'

As events headed towards what would turn out to be their bloody climax, Husbands and Estelle, with the approval of the governor of Texas, finally agreed to bring an armoured car into the prison yard. Just before 10pm on 3 August, the armed convicts embarked on their escape bid. At the suggestion of one of the hostages they put together a makeshift structure which consisted of wheeled chalkboards padded by substantial volumes from the library. Within its shelter Carrasco handcuffed himself to librarian Yvonne Beseda, and Dominguez and Cuevas fastened themselves to two other hostages. The rest of the hostages were secured to the outside to act as a human shield. Although neither Carrasco nor his captives knew it, Estelle was still intent on preventing any escape. As they all approached the armoured vehicle which was supposed to take them out of the prison, he ordered his men to turn powerful fire hoses on the homemade shield. The idea was to topple it over and free all the hostages in the ensuing chaos but the plan went badly wrong. Not only did the blast of water fail to overturn the shield, one of the hoses burst. Carrasco and his men began to fire their guns and the law officers responded in kind. Within a short space of time, Yvonne Beseda and another hostage, Julia Standley, were killed, Carrasco committed suicide by turning his gun on himself, and Dominguez was shot dead by prison guards. The surviving captor, Cuevas, spent nearly 17 years on Death Row before he was executed on 23 May 1991. His last words were, 'I'm going to a beautiful place. OK, warden, roll 'em'.

'None of us who were there for those eleven incredible days,' a TV reporter later said, 'will ever forget the tension, the heat, the frustration, and the courage of so many good people, inside and outside that prison. It is a tragedy that two hostages died. It is a miracle that all the rest lived.'

August

Faced with probable impeachment as a consequence of the Watergate scandal, the American president, Richard Nixon, resigns. A French high-wire artist walks between the two towers of the World Trade Center. In Yugoslavia, a train crash in Zagreb takes the lives of more than 150 people. Proto-punk band The Ramones play their first gig in New York's legendary CBGB club and a free music festival in Britain ends in chaos. Court Line Aviation goes bust and tens of thousands of British holidaymakers are stranded abroad.

Nixon Resigns

Beneath its innumerable complications and ramifications, the Watergate scandal that plagued Richard Nixon's second term as US president was essentially a simple story. In the early hours of 17 June 1972, five men were arrested at the Watergate Complex, a mixture of offices, apartments and hotel accommodation in Washington DC. They were all members of a team assigned to the Committee to Re-elect the President (CRP or, as it was more frequently described in the media, CREEP) and they were caught in the act of breaking into the offices of the Democratic National Committee in order to steal documents and plant surveillance devices. All the problems that ensued came from attempts to cover up these basic facts. The cover-up gradually compromised more and more members of the administration until it reached the very highest level and the president himself came under media scrutiny. Two relentless investigative reporters, Bob Woodward and Carl Bernstein, working for *The Washington Post*, refused to accept the stories they were being fed and persisted in digging ever deeper in search of the truth. They were pointed in the right direction by an informant they named 'Deep Throat' (after the title of a notorious porn movie of the time), many years later revealed to be a senior FBI man called Mark Felt.

Nixon was re-elected for a second term as president in November 1972 at a time when Watergate must have seemed to him no more than a minor irritation that would eventually disappear. However, the next eighteen months saw a series of revelations that piled increasing pressure on the president and his closest lieutenants. In May 1973, a Senate committee was established, its proceedings to be televised nationally as it attempted to unearth the full facts behind the developing scandal. A distinguished lawyer, Archibald Cox, a former Solicitor-General under President Kennedy, was appointed as a special prosecutor, charged with examining the possibility of presidential improprieties. By midsummer the existence of audiotapes recording Nixon's conversations and phone calls in the White House was known. Nixon then ordered the taping system to be abandoned and refused to hand over the tapes that already existed to Cox. Instead he engineered the special prosecutor's sacking and his replacement with someone the president hoped (vainly, as it turned out) would be more tractable.

In November 1973, Nixon delivered his now notorious answer to a press question in which he declared, 'people have got to know whether or not their president is a crook' and then, after a slight pause for emphasis, said, 'Well, I am not a crook'. As Watergate continued to dominate the news agenda throughout the rest of 1973 and into 1974, these words seemed increasingly hollow and, indeed, untrue. Each new revelation threatened to prove more of the president's complicity in the cover-up, and in the cover-up of the cover-up. Various members of his close circle were formally indicted for conspiracy, perjury and the obstruction of justice. The existence of the White House tapes continued to take centre stage. The release of edited transcripts of them at the end of April did little to halt the demand for the truth. Unedited versions, it was assumed, would provide unequivocal evidence of the president's direct involvement in criminal activities. Woodward and Bernstein published their book *All the President's Men* in June and, on 24 July, the Supreme Court ordered Nixon to surrender the tape recordings of the White House conversations about Watergate. Moves were now being made by Congress to impeach the president.

By August, it was clear that the game was up. Nixon had told his family that he was planning to resign on the second of that month but he was persuaded to reconsider the decision. However, the release of tapes three days later which revealed beyond argument that he had known of the White House link to the Watergate break-in soon after it had occurred, and that he had undoubtedly connived in the cover-up, meant the end of the road for him. 'This was the final blow, the final nail in the coffin,' Nixon told a former aide some years later. 'Although you don't need another nail if you're already in the coffin – which we were.' A delegation of senior Republicans from the Senate and the House of Representatives visited him to report that he was undoubtedly facing impeachment. (At that time, the only president who had been challenged in this way was Andrew Johnson more than a century earlier.) If impeachment went ahead, Nixon would almost certainly be found guilty and removed from office. His only choice was to resign with whatever dignity he could muster.

On 9 August, he did exactly that. As was required by legislation dating back to the 1790s, his resignation letter was sent to the Secretary of State, Henry Kissinger. For such a momentous communication, it was extraordinarily brief and to the point. 'Dear Mr Secretary,' it read, 'I hereby resign the Office of President of the United States.

Sincerely, Richard Nixon.' The previous evening he had taken his seat at his desk in the Oval Office to give his final televised address to the nation as its president. Earlier, as his makeup had been applied in preparation for this appearance, he had been in tears. Now he was composed as he began his speech with the blandly factual statement, 'This is the 37th time I have spoken to you from this office'. Few people who had been paying attention over previous months would have been greatly surprised that, as he continued, Nixon still refused to acknowledge any real responsibility for Watergate and the cover-up. The most he was prepared to say was that, 'if some of my judgments were wrong, and some *were* wrong, they were made in what I believed at the time to be the best interest of the nation'. He even attempted to present his impending resignation as an act of semi-heroic self-sacrifice. 'I have never been a quitter,' he said. 'To leave office before my term is completed is abhorrent to every instinct in my body. But as president, I must put the interest of America first.' As his address drew to its conclusion, he claimed that his period in office had given him 'a very personal sense of kinship with each and every American', and ended with a prayer: 'May God's grace be with you all in the days ahead.'

He then made his way to his living quarters in the White House, at first accompanied by Kissinger who assured him that history would remember him as a great president. 'That will depend on who writes the history,' Nixon is said to have replied. He stayed up until nearly 2 in the morning before catching a few hours of sleep in preparation for his day of exit. After signing his letter to Kissinger, he went with his family to make his farewells to

White House staff. With the sounds of 'Hail to the Chief', the American president's personal anthem, ringing in his ears for the last time, he was greeted by a three-minute ovation from the 300 people gathered in the East Room. 'We leave with high hopes, in good spirits and with deep humility, and with very much gratefulness in our hearts,' he told them before heading towards the South Lawn and the presidential helicopter. As he climbed aboard, Nixon turned briefly and gave his standard salute, both arms raised and two fingers on each hand making a 'V for victory' sign. 'The last that we saw of him as president,' a reporter from the *Guardian* wrote, 'was his limp right hand flapping occasionally like a dying fish, trying to wave a laconic farewell through the bulletproof glass of the shiny green helicopter.'

High-Wire Act

Born in Nemours in northern France in 1949, Philippe Petit developed an overwhelming interest in magic and juggling as a teenager before he was introduced to the art of the high wire. He was immediately entranced and it became his obsession. Petit first hit the headlines in June 1971, when he succeeded in placing a tightrope between the two towers of Notre Dame de Paris. Walking as easily along his wire 225 feet above ground as most of us take a morning stroll, he juggled balls and responded cheerfully to the applause of spectators below. In the summer of 1973, he was in the news once more after performing a similar feat at Sydney Harbour Bridge.

However, these performances were mere tasters for what was to come when Petit undertook his most attention-grabbing stunt by far. This came on the morning of 7 August 1974, when he performed a series of routines on a high wire strung between the two towers of New York's World Trade Center. It was something he had been planning in his mind since he was a teenager and had first read in a French newspaper about the project to construct the towers.

'Here I am,' he later recalled, 'young, 17-years-old, with a bad tooth in one of those uncolourful waiting rooms of a French dentist... suddenly, I freeze because I have opened a newspaper at a page and I see something magnificent, something that inspires me. I see two towers and the article says one day those towers will be built.'

The stunt had taken a long time to prepare. His first sight of the Twin Towers in reality rather than photographs was chastening. 'The minute I got out of the subway, climbing the steps, looking at them,' he said later, 'I knew that they were no dream. I knew that my dream was destroyed instantly... Impossible, impossible, impossible.' However, Petit recovered from his shock and persisted in his plan. Together with associates, he made dozens of visits to the Twin Towers to reconnoitre and to smuggle in the equipment and ropes he needed to set up the wire. He even built a scale model of the buildings in order to help him design the rigging he would need. He had an inside man in the form of one Barry Greenhouse who had an office on the 82nd floor of the south tower. On the night before the walk, Petit and a group of co-conspirators, dressed as construction workers, made their way past guards, intent on taking the bulk of the equipment, including the wire itself, into Greenhouse's office. From there they were able to reach the top of the tower. Now they faced the problem of getting the wire across to the other tower. The plan was to shoot an arrow over the gap, attached to a length of fishing line. This could then be used to string ever stronger support wires across the abyss and finally put in place the steel cable on which he was about to risk his life. Just after dawn, at around 7am, preparations were complete and Petit took his first steps on to the wire.

More than 1,300 feet above the ground, he performed a series of manoeuvres on the wire over the next 45 minutes, to the varying delight, horror and amazement of onlookers. 'Balance bar in hand,' one newspaper reported, 'he strode the 140-foot long steel cable, then decided to do tricks – prancing, bending down on one knee, running back and forth, even lying down.' Traffic came to a halt on the Brooklyn Bridge. The streets around the Trade Center filled with people, their eyes uplifted to the tiny figure on the wire above them. The authorities were less impressed than the crowds. Police officers arrived on the roofs of both towers to persuade him to abandon his performance. There was talk of a helicopter coming to snatch him from the wire, which would probably have been more of a threat to his safety than allowing him to continue. Petit finally decided to end his daredevil display after 45 minutes. He was arrested as he stepped down from his wire and initially charged with disorderly conduct and criminal trespass. The Manhattan District Attorney later offered to drop the case if Petit would put on a free (and legal) performance of his skills in Central Park. The aerialist agreed.

In the fifty years since, Petit's daring performance has been celebrated in a variety of media, from a prizewinning children's book (*The Man Who Walked Between the Towers* by Mordicai Gerstein) to *Man on Wire*, an acclaimed documentary film, and *The Walk*, a 2015 Hollywood movie, directed by Robert Zemeckis and starring Joseph Gordon-Levitt as Petit. A reporter once asked the real Petit why he had undertaken his legendary high-wire walk. 'There is no why,' Petit replied. 'If I see three oranges, I have to juggle. If I see two towers, I have to walk.'

The Ramones Play their First Gig at CBGB

One of the most influential bands of the 1970s was formed in the New York borough of Queens early in 1974. John Cummings and Thomas Erdelyi knew one another from their time together in a high-school band called the Tangerine Puppets, which had played a few gigs in 1966 and 1967. Douglas Colvin met and bonded with both Cummings and Erdelyi over a shared taste in music in the early 1970s. Together with Jeff Hyman, who had been singing with a band called Sniper, they became the four founding members of the Ramones.

Colvin had already decided to call himself Dee Dee Ramone, taking the name, it was said, from a pseudonym ('Paul Ramon') which Paul McCartney had employed in the early days of The Beatles. 'It's a nice name,' he told an interviewer in 1975. 'It just sounds nice.' The others followed suit. Cummings became Johnny Ramone, Erdelyi Tommy Ramone and Hyman Joey Ramone.

The Ramones' first time in front of an audience had been earlier in the year but their breakthrough performance came on 16 August at the club CBGB in Manhattan's East Village. The letters in the club's name had initially stood for Country, Blue Grass and Blues but CBGB rapidly became one of the centres for a new wave of rock music, soon to be dubbed 'punk'. Talking Heads, Blondie and Patti Smith were just some of the famous names who, in the words of music journalist Everett True, 'honed their stagecraft there with its tiny stage and legendarily foul toilets'. The place had other advantages. As True goes on to say in his biography of the Ramones, 'It was cheap. The bands were cheap. The beer was cheap. The punters were cheap. The groupies were plentiful.'

According to Hilly Kristal, the legendary owner of CBGB, the Ramones initially 'were the most un-together band I'd ever heard. They kept starting and stopping – equipment breaking down... They were a mess.' He recalled that they'd 'play for 40 minutes... and 20 of them would just be the band yelling at each other'. Despite (or perhaps because of) their wild unpredictability, they were popular. They went on to play at CBGB another 22 times before the end of the year. Their repertoire of what one music writer called 'short, furious songs played at terrifying speed' proved highly influential. The late Joe Strummer, frontman for the Clash, described the Ramones as 'the daddy punk group of all time'. It was not until 1976 that their debut studio album, *Ramones*, was released, to be followed by a further 13 over the next 19 years. They appeared in the 1979 film *Rock 'n' Roll High School*, performing the title track, and had a brief, ill-starred collaboration with legendary, indeed infamous, producer Phil Spector. After more than 2,250 concert performances, they disbanded, playing their last show on 6 August 1996 in Los Angeles. All four of the original Ramones (Joey, Dee Dee, Johnny and Tommy) have now passed away but their musical legacy lives on and, in a sense, it began one night in August 1974 in a club in Manhattan.

Holidaymakers Stranded

The 1960s and the 1970s were the decade in which package holidays abroad really took off in Britain. Millions of ordinary people, who had never previously been much further than their nearest seaside town, found that they were able to afford to head for Spain and the Balearic Islands, and that travel companies and cheap airlines were happy to take them. Resorts such as Benidorm and Torremelinos became as familiar to many holidaymakers as Blackpool and Scarborough. 1974 was the year in which that kitschy anthem to sun, sea and holiday romance, 'Y Viva Espana' (actually written by a Belgian and sung by the Swedish Sylvia Vrethammar), spent weeks in the UK Singles Chart. However, it was also the year in which Court Line Aviation went bust, stranding many thousands of British holidaymakers in foreign places.

Court Line had begun life as a shipping business in the first decade of the twentieth century and moved into charter aviation in the 1960s, buying a company called Autair. By 1974, in conjunction with the travel firm Clarksons Holidays, which it had taken over, it was one of the biggest operators in the ever-growing package holiday business. It had achieved this status through innovation and a willingness to try things that staider airlines would never do. Their fleet of BAC1-11s was painted in a variety of attractive pastel colours. The female cabin crew wore uniforms designed by Mary Quant, creator in the 1960s of the mini-skirt. Food was provided in boxes attached to the seats in front to which customers could help themselves when they wanted, although they might have been disappointed to discover that they often contained little more than spam sandwiches.

The airline may have been adopting new ideas but it was also, although few people knew it, teetering on the brink of bankruptcy. For a variety of reasons, from the huge rises in the cost of oil to people's awareness of everyday inflation, holiday bookings, which had been more or less continually increasing in number during the previous decade, actually went down in 1974. Court Line had not planned well for this and was in difficulties. By 13 August, the Foreign Secretary, Jim Callaghan, was warning British embassies around the world that there was trouble ahead. Two days later, Court Line went into liquidation. All its flights were cancelled, its planes were grounded, 1,500 employees lost their jobs overnight and tens of thousands of holidaymakers who had had the bad luck to book their trips to the sun with Court Line and Clarksons found themselves unsure how they were going to get home.

In addition, many more thousands had holidays booked through Clarksons and had already paid in advance. There were angry scenes at the company's London offices where a cordon of police had to be formed to prevent furious customers breaking in to a board meeting with demands to know why money had continued to be taken from them when the directors must have been aware of looming disaster. Dramatic headlines in the newspapers suggested that some Brits might be in for a long wait before they saw home again. In reality, the missions to rescue those stuck in Spain and more than 20 other countries were, for the most part, very successful. Many people who were halfway through their holidays were able to finish them and catch other flights home with no difficulties. Money was found to fund the return of those stranded but not enough to refund nearly 100,000 people who had paid in advance for their vacations. The Court Line collapse resulted in significant changes to ensure that tourists would never have to endure quite such inconveniences and financial losses in the future.

ABTA, the Association of British Travel Agents, improved its consumer protection scheme and, the following year, legislation was passed in the form of the Air Travel Reserve Fund Act 1975 to make certain that money would be available to refund travellers who had paid up front for holidays that were lost in similar circumstances.

Windsor Free Festival

In the summer of 1974, a free festival of music was planned for Windsor Great Park, once common land below Windsor Castle but which had long ago been taken over by the Crown Estate. The event would, in effect, be taking place in the royal backyard. This was the third such festival. The principal organiser was the Irish anarchist and counter-culture activist Ubi Dwyer. The first had been two years previously and, despite Dwyer's attempts to publicise it, had not been a marked success. Fewer than a thousand people turned up and the festival came to an end much sooner than Dwyer and his friends had hoped. Undeterred, he tried again in the summer of 1973. Just as in the previous year, he didn't bother with trivial formalities like seeking permission from the Crown Estate. 'The festival... is a revolution,' he told a local newspaper. 'We want a new society.' The Crown Estate didn't and it banned the festival in advance. The ban had little noticeable effect and this time there was a much better attendance. Estimates of the numbers there range from 10 to 20 thousand. Many of them stayed for nine days. Police were also there in force and there were several ugly confrontations between them and festivalgoers. Almost 300 arrests were made, mostly for drug offences.

The third Windsor Free Festival was scheduled to last ten days but it came to an abrupt end on the sixth morning, Wednesday 28 August. The police had been a significant presence from the beginning. They had erected metal barriers in an attempt to keep vehicles out. (Earlier plans to surround the site with barbed wire or even flood it temporarily with sewage had been abandoned.) Officers were everywhere. 'When we began to walk down to the festival site itself the number of police lining the roadside was just HUGE,' one attendee remembered. 'There seemed to be a policeman every fifty feet or so.' Undercover police mingled with the crowds, although they 'could be spotted a mile off as they had such short hair and crappy clothes'.

The man in charge of the policing, Chief Constable David Holdsworth, had soon seen enough. In his mind the festival was 'nothing more than a gigantic drug-inspired breach of the peace'. As he told the official enquiry the following year, 'I changed my mind about containing it and decided to bring it to an end'. Hundreds of Thames Valley police officers invaded the site and attendees were given a mere ten minutes in which to depart. Large numbers of them did not and the police proceeded to act in an astonishingly aggressive fashion. 'The police... ploughed into the crowd,' one witness reported. 'The front line of police had truncheons drawn and were swinging them viciously at anyone who got in their way.' Several hundred festivalgoers were arrested, often with little justification. 'I don't know why the police got so violent,' one witness told a BBC reporter. 'People were being thrown into police vans for no reason.'

The newspapers in the days after the violent end to the Windsor festival were, perhaps surprisingly, sympathetic to those who had been there for what the *Times* called 'the languid pursuit of music and sunshine'. 'Were the Police Too Tough?' was the question asked by a *Sun* headline, apparently expecting the answer, 'Yes'. The writer in the *Times* concluded by arguing that festivals were 'basically amiable gatherings, which with a degree of tolerance it should be possible to accommodate'. George Melly, writing in a Sunday newspaper a few days later, mourned what he saw as the end of the alternative culture of the 1960s. 'The last bastion... was that free festival in Windsor last week and... the law moved in with truncheons and shut the whole thing down.'

Zagreb Train Disaster

What has been described as the worst rail accident in Croatian history occurred in 1974. At about 7.45pm on 30 August, an express train, heading from Belgrade in what was then Yugoslavia to Dortmund in West Germany, approached Zagreb's main station, travelling at more than 40mph in excess of the speed limit for that stretch of track. It failed to slow down for a red signal. The drivers, suddenly realising the danger, desperately applied the brakes but it was far too late. Although the locomotive at the front remained on the tracks, all nine carriages behind it derailed and several of them overturned completely.

Of the 400 passengers on board, at least 153 people were killed. (Some reports put the death toll even higher.) As many as 40 of them were so badly mangled in the crash that they could not be identified. Unclaimed by any family members, they were buried in a common grave in Zagreb's Mirogoj Cemetery where there is now a monument to the victims of the crash, the work of a renowned Yugoslav sculptor named Vojin Bakić. Most of those killed in the accident were Yugoslav *gastarbeiter*, migrant workers to Germany, who had been returning to the area in which they worked after spending a summer break in their home country. Many of them had wives and children with them. According to survivors, the express had been travelling far too fast long before it approached the station. 'At least two hours before Zagreb, I told my husband, "We are going to jump the tracks",' one woman said to a reporter as she was lying in her hospital bed.

The following day, 31 August, was declared a national day of mourning. Then it was up to the authorities to discover how and why the tragedy had occurred. In the immediate aftermath of the crash, blood samples were taken from the driver and the rest of the crew to discover whether or not they had been drinking but it soon became apparent that, although one passenger was quoted as saying 'the driver must have been drunk or crazy', it was not alcohol that was to blame for the disaster. It was tiredness. At the enquiry into the disaster, the driver and his assistant claimed that the brakes had failed but crash investigators successfully argued that this could not have been the case. In further tests it became clear that, had the train been travelling at the recommended speed, the accident would not have happened. The two men were arraigned for manslaughter and both admitted during the course of their trial that they had fallen asleep. The fact that they had been suffering from exhaustion after working for 52 consecutive hours provided extenuating circumstances but they were sentenced to terms of imprisonment, the driver for 15 years and his assistant for 8.

September

Haile Selassie, emperor of Ethiopia, is deposed after 44 years on the throne. In the USA, President Gerald Ford provides his predecessor Richard Nixon with a 'full, free and absolute pardon' for any wrongdoings in office. A TWA flight from Tel-Aviv to New York is blown from the skies. Two pandas arrive at London Zoo, a gift from the Chinese government. A Native American tribe declares war on the American government and wins a significant victory. Daredevil Evel Knievel attempts to jump the Snake River Canyon on a rocket-powered motorcycle. In Spain, Basque separatists bomb a Madrid café.

Haile Selassie Deposed

By 1974, Haile Selassie had been emperor of Ethiopia for more than four decades. Tafari Makonnen, as he was originally known, was born into an aristocratic family, one which claimed to be able to trace its lineage back to a son of King Solomon and the Queen of Sheba, on 23 July 1892. He became emperor in 1930, taking the name by which he is now best known, which translates as 'Might of the Trinity'. He was forced into exile following the Italian invasion of his country six years later, spending much of this time in a house in the English spa city of Bath. In January 1941, he was able to return to Ethiopia when a joint Ethiopian and British force retook the country after a campaign lasting several months and reinstated him as emperor. During the years that followed, he undertook a variety of reforms - social, economic and educational - in an effort to modernise the country without ever relinquishing any of his personal power. Opposition to his regime occasionally emerged - dissident soldiers briefly took control of parts of his capital, Addis Ababa, in 1960, for example - but was quickly quashed.

By the 1970s, after four decades in power, Haile Selassie, once the champion of reform in his country, had become the obstacle that stood in the way of further modernisation. The coup that finally unseated him had been evolving slowly throughout much of the year. Both the civilian population and the military, on whom the emperor's continuing power ultimately depended, had been growing restive. Strikes and student agitation had hit the nation's capital, Addis Ababa, in February. Towards the end of the same month, the emperor himself had to intervene to quell a minor mutiny of soldiers in the city, visiting them in their headquarters to promise a pay increase and better conditions. However, further mutinies broke out in garrisons across the country and student demonstrations continued. By the end of February, Selassie's entire cabinet of ministers had resigned and the army was effectively in control of Addis Ababa.

The emperor appointed a new prime minister in the Oxford-educated Endalkatchew Makonnen whose father had held the same position two decades earlier. Makonnen advocated reforms that would have transformed Ethiopia into, in effect, a constitutional monarchy but both he and the emperor remained blind to growing dangers to the very existence of the regime. 'After March,' as one historian of the country wrote, 'the direction was toward revolution.' At the end of June, the Coordinating Committee of the Armed Forces, usually known as the *derg*, the Amharic word for 'committee', was created. Although the *derg* issued repeated assurances of loyalty to the emperor in the next two months, in reality it was working to undermine all the institutions on which the monarchy's foundations rested. Makonnen was forced out of power in July and replaced by a man who was little more than the *derg*'s puppet. Early on the morning of 12 September, a small group of officers arrived at the palace. Dressed in full uniform, Haile Selassie heard one of them, speaking with noticeable nervousness, read out a proclamation of deposition. The emperor agreed to stand down as the country's ruler in the best interests of its people and was escorted from the palace to be taken to one of the army's headquarter buildings.

In the aftermath of the revolution, the Polish journalist Ryszard Kapuscinski interviewed former members of the court, many of them in hiding and in fear for their lives. What was revealed was a court that, for all Haile Selassie's reforming zeal as a younger ruler, had been almost feudal in its rituals and ceremonies. Some of those Kapuscinski interviewed had very specific tasks that they had to perform in order to fulfil protocol and ensure the emperor's comfort. One man, identified only as AM-M, was keeper of the third door in the Audience Hall. His chief job was to open this door at the precise moment required to allow Haile Selassie to leave the hall without compromising his 'lordly dignity' by having to slow his walking pace or (heaven forbid!) come to a halt. Another, GS-D, was 'His Most Virtuous Highness's pillow-bearer for twenty-six years'. Haile Selassie was a short man with a high throne and there was always the danger that his legs might dangle unbecomingly in the air. GS-D's task was to slide a pillow beneath the imperial footwear to ensure that this never happened.

The court, and the country's capital, was also a place of endless intrigue, backstabbing and conspiracy. 'The palace divided itself into factions and coteries that fought incessant wars,' one interviewee stated, 'weakening and destroying one another.' The courtiers all lived in an atmosphere of fear and distrust. 'They had no shield but the Emperor, and the Emperor could undo them with one wave of his hand.' They were all dependent on Haile Selassie's whim. 'His Majesty never made appointments on the basis of a man's talents, but always and exclusively on the basis of loyalty,' another interviewee reported. As a consequence, 'the fight for a piece of the Emperor's ear never stopped'. The wonder is not that the Ethiopian revolution took place but that the regime lasted as long as it did.

Haile Selassie survived the coup that overthrew him by less than a year. The former emperor died in August 1975, aged 83. The official cause of death was respiratory failure as a result of complications from a prostate operation. Rumours that he had, in fact, been strangled in his bed proliferated but seem unlikely to have been true.

Ford Pardons Nixon

Following Richard Nixon's resignation in August (see page 153), the vice-president Gerald Ford stepped into his shoes. At his swearing-in ceremony, the new president had declared, 'My fellow Americans, our long national nightmare is over'. He was being over-optimistic. The shadow of Nixon and the Watergate scandal would not disappear overnight. It still hung over the government and the nation's perception of the honesty and trustworthiness of its lawmakers. One of the first problems Ford had to face as president was what to do about his predecessor. He addressed it in a televised speech on 8 September. 'I have come to a decision,' he told his audience, 'which I felt I should tell you and all of my fellow American citizens, as soon as I was certain in my own mind and in my own conscience that it is the right thing to do.'

The decision to which he had come was a simple one. It was to grant Nixon 'a full, free and absolute pardon'. Nixon's resignation the previous month had been forced upon him by the relentless Watergate revelations and by the growing threat that, if he didn't go, he would be impeached. Ford had only been Nixon's vice-president for eight months. He had replaced Spiro Agnew who had been obliged to tender his own resignation the previous year because he was facing charges of income tax evasion and corruption.

As Ford correctly stated, 'There are no historic or legal precedents to which I can turn in this matter...' However, when he went on to say of the Nixons that 'theirs is an American tragedy in which we have all played a part', he was on less certain ground. Many in his audience might have debated the use of the word 'tragedy' in connection with Nixon and wondered quite how everybody in America had played a part in the former president's covering up of a crime and then lying persistently about his own involvement in that cover-up. Fewer people watching would have disputed Ford's next words. 'It could go on and on and on, or someone must write the end to it. I have concluded that only I can do that, and if I can, I must.'

Within ten minutes of Ford finishing his address, Nixon had released his own statement, thanking the new president for his 'compassionate act' and claiming that 'no words can describe the depths of my regret and pain at the anguish my mistakes over Watergate have caused the nation and the presidency'. Nixon's feelings about the pardon were necessarily ambivalent. Yes, he had been saved any further humiliations and the very real possibility of a criminal trial. However, a full, free and absolute pardon implied that there had been serious wrongdoing and Nixon could never quite accept that he had been guilty of much more than mere 'mistakes' in his Watergate actions. 'Next to the resignation,' he later wrote, 'accepting the pardon was the most painful decision of my political career.'

In the nation at large, the pardon was, of course, deeply controversial. In the *New York Times*, it was described as a 'profoundly unwise, divisive, and unjust act'. The new president's approval ratings, initially high, plummeted. One close ally, the journalist Jerald terHorst, whom Ford had appointed a month earlier as his press secretary, resigned in protest at the decision. 'Try as I can,' he wrote in his resignation letter, 'it is impossible to conclude that the former president is more deserving of mercy than persons of lesser station in life whose offenses have had far less effect on our national well-being.' Many historians of the period believe that the granting of the pardon was, at the very least, a contributing factor to Ford's defeat by Jimmy Carter in the 1976 presidential election.

TWA *Flight 841*

TWA Flight 841 took off from Ben Gurion International Airport in Tel Aviv on Sunday 8 September on a regularly scheduled flight to John F. Kennedy Airport in New York. It landed first at Athens where some passengers left and others joined. After just over an hour at the Greek airport, the plane took off for Rome where it would make one final stop before heading across the Atlantic. After leaving the Greek mainland behind, the pilot reported that one engine was on fire and that he was intending to make for Corfu in the hope of undertaking an emergency landing there. Very shortly afterwards, ground controllers lost contact with the plane.

About half an hour after leaving Athens, some 50 nautical miles west of the island of Cephalonia, TWA Flight 841 plunged into the Ionian Sea, killing all 79 passengers and 9 crew members. The disaster was witnessed by crew on the flight deck of another aircraft who reported that the plane had first undertaken a steep climb in the skies before an engine had clearly fallen from its wing. Immediately after this, Flight 841 had flipped over on its back and then entered a steep, spiralling descent to its doom in the sea below. Rescue services in both Greece and Brindisi, the nearest Italian city, were alerted but ships operating in the area were first on the scene. Debris was floating on the surface of the sea but there were no signs of any survivors.

At first, despite a claim of responsibility by a Palestinian organisation, it was thought unlikely that the crash was the result of sabotage. However, further investigation by the American National Transportation Safety Board proved that there had indeed been a bomb hidden in the plane's hold. Its explosion had destroyed the cables controlling the aircraft's rudder system which had caused it to crash. A later examination by a team of British bomb experts found two tiny fragments of metal embedded in a suitcase recovered from the wreckage. Scientific analysis showed that the speed at which these metallic bits had hit the bag could only have been the result of a bomb exploding. It has been suggested that Abu Nidal, head of the most ruthless Palestinian terrorist group in the 1970s and 1980s, may have been implicated in the destruction of Flight 841 but this suspicion has never been definitively confirmed.

Pandas at London Zoo

By September 1974, London Zoo had been without giant pandas for its visitors to admire for more than two years. (The previous panda, Chi Chi, had been one of the zoo's star attractions for many years but had died in July 1972.) On the 14th of the month two replacements for her flew in from China, courtesy of Mao Zedong's government. They were sent as a gift to Ted Heath following his successful visit to the country in May 1974, soon after he had been ousted from Downing Street and become Leader of the Opposition. China had long made use of what has been dubbed 'panda diplomacy' and the present of Ching-Ching and Chia-Chia marked a thawing of the UK's relationship with Communist China.

Initially, the zoo was not entirely delighted by the prospect of the pandas' arrival. It was expected to pay Ching-Ching's and Chia-Chia's airfares and this was no small sum. Lord Zuckerman, then Secretary of the London Zoological Society, even paid the prime minister a visit in which, according to a civil servant who was present, he said that 'being the agent for demonstrations of friendship between the British and Chinese governments was proving to be a pretty expensive business'. The new arrivals, like all giant pandas, proved fussy eaters, insisting only on a special kind of bamboo which was despatched to them by train from Cornwall twice a week. The zoo also had to provide two white rhinos to send to China as a reciprocal present from Britain. High maintenance though they were, the pandas soon showed they were worth it. In the weeks after they came to the zoo, attendance doubled.

Since Ching-Ching was female and Chia-Chia male the hope was that they might mate but this began to fade when the pair showed no romantic interest in one another. 'Theirs is a life of eating and sleeping,' one keeper at the zoo noted, and they seemed to have no time for anything else. After many years in which neither panda displayed any amorous intent, the zoo decided desperate measures were demanded. In 1981, while Chia-Chia had a sabbatical in Washington DC, in the hope that he might mate successfully with another female there (he didn't), Ching-Ching was artificially inseminated. For a while it seemed as if this had worked and the zoo announced that she might be pregnant. As more and more visitors flocked to see her, plans were made to install closed circuit television to record the moment of birth. Unfortunately, it all turned out to be a false alarm and a false pregnancy. Ching-Ching was destined never to be a mother. She died of peritonitis in 1985. Chia-Chia was sent to Mexicó to join another panda breeding programme where he finally fathered several offspring. He died in 1991.

Cafeteria Rolando Bombing in Spain

The assassination in December 1973 of Luis Carrero Blanco, prime minister and longtime confidant of General Franco, dubbed 'Operation Ogre' by its perpetrators, rocked Spanish society and emphasised the increasing fragility of the Franco regime. A further shock to the system came on 13 September in the following year when a bomb exploded in the Cafeteria Rolando. Situated on the Calle del Correo, the café had been targeted because it was close to the headquarters of the Spanish police, many of whom were its customers. The bomb, which consisted of 30 kilos of dynamite packed with metallic nuts to act as shrapnel, blew up just after 2.30pm in the entrance to the café. The building was seriously damaged. The café ceiling collapsed. People on the first floor fell through it and into the ground-floor café. Cars parked in the street were destroyed. A dozen people, including a newly married couple and two employees of the cafe, were killed instantly and more than 70 wounded. Not one of the 12 was actually a police officer, although Inspector Felix Pinel suffered bad head injuries which led to his death two years later. The Cafeteria Rolando bombing was the first such indiscriminate terrorist attack that Spain had seen since the end of the Civil War more than three decades earlier.

The atrocity was assumed to be the work of the Basque separatist group ETA ('Euskadi Ta Askatasuna' which translates roughly as 'Basque Country and Freedom'), although it did not, as it had done for the murder of Carrero Blanco, claim responsibility at the time. The absence of any immediate admission of guilt by anyone, and the fact that no police officers had been amongst those initially killed in the blast, fuelled conspiracy theories. Had the bomb been planted, some people wondered, by extreme right-wing elements in the police force itself? Rumours spread that an internal circular within police headquarters had warned officers not to eat at the restaurant that day. In reality, as with most conspiracy theories, there was little evidence to back up such claims and, although no police officer died at the scene, several were badly injured, including the second-in-command of the Francoist political police.

In the months following the bombing, internal dissensions within ETA triggered a split within the organisation between those who were prepared to countenance more such actions and those who believed that they were counter-productive. The authorities moved swiftly to arrest known sympathisers with ETA. Amongst those imprisoned for alleged complicity in the bombing was Eva Forest, a political writer and the wife of Alfonso Sastre, one of the leading Spanish playwrights of the twentieth century, a fierce critic of Franco's regime. She was kept in prison until 1977 when an amnesty was declared for all political prisoners incarcerated during Franco's rule. There are still plenty of unanswered questions about the Cafeteria Rolando bombing, and it was only as recently as 2018 that one wing of ETA belatedly acknowledged involvement. It seems likely that the bomb was left in the café by two young Basques who had entered as customers, left the device, connected to a timer, under a table and departed.

The Kootenai War

On 20 September the 67 members of the Kootenai tribe from Idaho formally declared war on the USA. It was a last bid to draw attention to their loss of land over the years and to the appalling conditions in which they were obliged to live. Houses that had been built in the 1930s were now dilapidated and exposed to the elements. Medical services and educational opportunities were poor to non-existent. The Kootenai wanted federal recognition as a tribe in order to access help to improve their lives. The trigger for their action was the death of a tribal elder, a victim of hypothermia, in his crumbling, unheated home. Led by a 38-year-old woman called Amy Trice, who had been elected tribal chairperson, the Kootenai decided that urgent measures were needed. A letter was written to the Bureau of Indian Affairs, asking for a grant to build new houses and a better road. The BIA replied that a tribe had to have at least 125 members to qualify for financial aid and there was nothing that they could do to help. In a last, desperate attempt to highlight their plight, the Kootenai made their declaration of war with the USA. 'So we said, "Let's go to war",' Trice remembered. 'We said it jokingly but it turned serious.' The war, unlike nearly every other war in history, involved little to no violence, although the threat of it was initially present. 'The state police came with mace and sawed-off shotguns,' Trice said. 'The closest thing we had to a weapon in our tribal office was a fly swatter.'

Instead of taking up arms, or even fly swatters, members of the community were sent to stand by US Highway 95 as it passed through tribal lands near the small township of Bonners Ferry. They held up hand-painted signs reading, 'Entering Kootenai Reservation, ten-cent toll'. Specially designed 'war bonds', signed by Trice, were issued. Money to support the tribe's action began to pour in, donations arriving from around the world as news of the 'war' spread.

The 1970s saw what one historian has called 'a wave of activism' by Native Americans wishing to assert tribal sovereignty and demand the rights guaranteed in previous treaties. In February 1973, more than 200 Oglala Sioux and members of the American Indian Movement had occupied the historically significant township of Wounded Knee. FBI agents, US Marshals, BIA policemen and a small army of other law enforcement officers surrounded the place and a stand-off ensued which lasted more than seventy days. Two of the Native American activists were shot and killed during the siege and a US Marshal suffered life-changing injuries in an exchange of gunfire. The authorities had no wish to see any repetition in Idaho of these events at Wounded Knee. The Kootenai 'war' was now serious enough to merit the attention of the new US president, Gerald Ford. After Amy Trice led a delegation to Washington DC, he put his name to a bill which granted the Kootenai twelve and a half acres of federal land to create a new reservation. Money was provided to build a road to the reservation and a community centre there. In addition, the authorities agreed to spend $7,000 per tribe member in improving conditions for the Kootenai.

In the decades since 1974, the numbers of Kootenai have more than doubled, a casino, opened in 1996, has brought them further income, and the tribe has become involved in a number of projects, including a fish hatchery, designed to benefit their community and its environs. Amy Trice, the driving force behind the 'war', went on to become a founding member of the Upper Columbia United Tribes and to work for other organisations which promoted Native American and women's rights. She died in 2011 at the age of 75. 'I'm hoping,' she once said, 'that my childen and grandchildren will know how at one time their grandmother was crazy.'

Evel Knievel Jumps Snake River Canyon

One of the great folk heroes of twentieth-century America, motorcycling daredevil Robert Craig Knievel was born in Butte, Montana in 1938 and brought up there. After leaving school in his teens, he had a variety of jobs including working in the local copper mines until he was dismissed for crashing an earthmover into the main power line for the entire city, leaving Butte without electricity for several hours. He turned to stunt-riding initially as a means of promoting a motorbike shop in which he had an interest. His earliest attempt to jump his bike over an obstacle, in 1965, involved two caged mountain lions and a box of rattlesnakes. It nearly went badly wrong when his back wheel hit the crate containing the snakes but Knievel was now hooked on the adrenaline rush, and financial potential, of motorcycle stunts. He formed his own troupe of performers and began to tour as 'Bobby Knievel and his Motorcycle Daredevils'. Knievel told various stories about how 'Bobby' became 'Evel'. The most likely tells of how a promoter early in his career thought that the troupe's name was too uninspiring. He suggested 'Evil Knievel and his Motorcycle Daredevils' as a more eye-catching alternative. Knievel agreed but, worried that the new name might suggest he was some kind of Hell's Angel, insisted that the spelling be changed from 'Evil' to 'Evel'.

June 1966 saw him undertake his first attempts to leap over a line of cars. On the 19th of that month, he aimed to clear 13 vehicles in Missoula, Montana but fell short, suffering a broken arm and broken ribs in the process. Knievel was launched (literally) on what was to prove a long, productive career of breaking bones and jumping motorcycles over assorted barriers. His first televised stunt came in March 1967 at the Ascot Park speedway track in the city of Gardena, California, when he successfully cleared 15 cars. Others followed and, by the end of the following year, he was ready, or so he thought, for Las Vegas. What was intended to be a spectacular jump over the fountains at Caesars Palace Hotel on 31 December was not entirely successful. Knievel cleared the fountains but made a hash of his landing. He fractured his skull and spent the next month in a coma.

This was not enough to dissuade him from his chosen path. He continued to crack ribs and break other bones in a series of jumps throughout the early 1970s. By September 1974, he was a nationwide celebrity. His next stunt, undertaken on the 8th of that month, was to be his most spectacular and risky yet. Snake River Canyon is in Idaho, where it forms part of the boundary between Twin Falls County to the south and Jerome County to the north. The distance between the two banks is around 1,600 feet. Knievel's idea was to soar over the canyon on a custom-built, rocket-powered Skycycle X-2 motorbike but, not for the first or last time in his career, all did not go according to plan. Using his 'Evel Knievel Freedom Crane', a star-spangled hoist designed to lower him in a dignified fashion on to his mount, the stuntman took his seat in the Skycycle and gave a thumbs-up to watching supporters.

Just after three-thirty in the afternoon, the rocket whooshed into action and Knievel and his machine were hurtled in the direction of the opposite bank. Unfortunately, before the Skycycle had even left its launch ramp, its parachute prematurely deployed. Caught by the wind, the rocket bike failed to reach the other side. Instead it was blown back to the bank from which it was launched and crashed into the canyon below. Knievel had to be dragged from the wreckage and helicoptered to safety. By his own standards, his injuries from the Snake River Canyon jump were minor – a broken nose and a variety of cuts and bruises.

Nonetheless his experience on the Skycycle marked the beginning of a slowing in his career as a daredevil. 1975 saw him try only two jumps. (He had undertaken eight in 1974 before his attempt on Snake River Canyon.) The first involving 13 single-decker buses was at London's Wembley Stadium. He landed on the thirteenth bus and, once more, had to be hauled off to hospital, this time with concussion and a fractured pelvis. The second, some months later, was over 14 Greyhound buses in an Ohio amusement park. He landed on the fourteenth bus but escaped any major injury. His final stunt came in Chicago in January 1977 when he tried literally to jump the shark. The idea was to propel his Harley-Davidson 90 feet over a pool filled with sharks but he crashed during a practice run and had to withdraw from the event.

Knievel's post-daredevil career was almost as eventful as his time as a stunt rider. After attacking a former associate with a baseball bat, shouting, 'I'm going to kill you,' he served six months in jail. His conviction lost him lucrative marketing deals, including one with Ideal Toys, a company which manufactured and sold $125 million worth of Evel Knievel figurines between 1972 and 1977. Declared bankrupt, he endured several years of obscurity before re-emerging as some kind of national folk hero, remembered and admired for his near-suicidal devotion to entertaining his fans by risking his neck on a motorbike. He died in Clearwater, Florida in November 2007. 'His fame had little to do with the stunts he successfully pulled off,' his biographer Stuart Barker has written, 'and everything to do with the epic failures and wipeouts.'

October

Oskar Schindler, the German factory owner who saved more than a thousand Jews from the gas chambers during the Second World War, dies at the age of 66. In Britain, the second general election of the year sees Labour gain the slimmest of majorities. The Provisional IRA bomb two pubs in Guildford. In the so-called 'Rumble in the Jungle', Muhammad Ali fights George Foreman for the heavyweight championship of the world. McDonald's opens its first restaurant in the UK in Woolwich.

Death of Oskar Schindler

Oskar Schindler, who died in West Germany on 9 October 1974, exemplified the sometimes forgotten truth that you don't have to be a plaster saint in order to do good in the world. Schindler was a drinker, a womaniser and a ruthless businessman with few scruples. Yet he was also someone prepared to risk his life to save hundreds of Jews from the Nazis during the Second World War. He was born in 1908 in Zwittau, now Svitavy in the Czech Republic but then part of the Austro-Hungarian Empire. A member of a pro-German party in Czechoslovakia in the mid-1930s, he was arrested by the Czech authorities for espionage in 1938 and sentenced to death but the annexation of the Sudetenland by the Nazis that year saved his life. He joined the Nazi Party in 1939, almost certainly as a means of advancing his financial prospects rather than because of any ideological commitment to the cause.

Following the German invasion of Poland, Schindler made his way to Krakow where he bought a factory and began employing Jewish workers in the industrial manufacture of pots and pans. By 1942, he had more than 400 at the factory, brought in each day from the ghetto created by the Nazis. The following year saw the appointment as commandant of the Krakow-Plaszow concentration camp of the sadistic psychopath Amon Göth, 'the most despicable man I have ever met', according to Schindler's wife, Emilie. Schindler was still to outward appearances a supporter of the Nazis and their plans for Poland. Through a mixture of charm, bribery and bonhomie, he succeeded in persuading Göth that he should be allowed to run a separate sub-camp solely for his workers at his Emalia factory, where he was able to protect them from the savagery and random murders at the main camp. During this period, Schindler was twice arrested for black market activities and once for breaking the Nuremberg Laws on racial purity by kissing a Jewish girl on the cheek during a birthday party for him at his factory. On the latter occasion, he spent five days in prison before his Nazi contacts were able to arrange for his release.

In July 1944, as the Red Army drew nearer, German concentration camps and factories in Eastern Europe were closing down. Prisoners and slave labourers were being sent west. Schindler's factory was one of those in line to be decommissioned but he successfully petitioned for it to be moved to Brünnlitz in the Sudetenland (now Brnenec in the Czech Republic). He compiled a list of his Jewish workers who were, he said, essential to the running of the factory, thus saving them from delivery to concentration camps and, in all likelihood, the gas chambers. By this time the factory was making shells for the Nazi war effort but Schindler, risking his life again, ensured that the shells were basically duds and didn't work.

When the war came to an end, he was initially thought, by those who did not know of his hidden activities on behalf of his workers, to be a Nazi war criminal. He was obliged to flee the country, helped to do so by some of the Jews he had earlier saved. In 1949, he moved to Argentina, hoping to rescue his fortune as a farmer but this was not a success. Bankrupt and divorced from his wife, he returned to Europe and died in Hildesheim in Lower Saxony, aged 66. His posthumous fame grew thanks to Thomas Keneally's novel *Schindler's Ark*, first published in 1982, and (most dramatically) through Steven Spielberg's 1993 film, *Schindler's List*, which was based on the book. He is buried in Jerusalem where he is hailed in Hebrew on his gravestone as 'Righteous Among the Nations' and described in a German inscription as 'The Unforgettable Lifesaver of 1,200 Persecuted Jews'. He had his own explanation for what he did. 'I hated the brutality, the sadism, and the insanity of Nazism,' he once said. 'I just couldn't stand by and see people destroyed. I did what I could, what I had to do, what my conscience told me to do. That's all there is to it. Really, nothing more.'

Second Election in UK

Given that the February election (see p. 37) in Britain had resulted in a hung parliament, it was inevitable that another would be needed sooner or later. The second one of the year took place on Thursday 10 October, less than eight months after the previous one. It was the first time since 1910 that the country had gone to the polls twice in the same year. Prime Minister Harold Wilson had announced his decision to go to the country again the previous month. It was time, he told the electorate in a TV address, for Labour to have a majority in order 'to make government and parliament work'. A coalition had been mooted as one way out of the impasse but Wilson was dismissive of that idea. The result would be 'fuzzy compromises' when what the nation needed were 'clear decisions'.

Few people seemed enthused by the idea of another chance to make their choice of MP. The *Times* was of the opinion that, since the war, no election had 'been held in such a mood of public uncertainty and depression'. It also suggested that this was an election that might 'damage or even destroy the party that wins it'. The campaign began with the encouraging news for the government that polls were predicting a Labour lead of 8 per cent, more than enough to grant them the House of Commons majority they wanted. They kept that lead throughout the weeks of campaigning that followed, with some polls suggesting that it had crept above 10 per cent.

Campaigning was low-key compared with other elections. *The Economist* called it 'the election that never was' and one Tory strategist, more than a week before polling day, was heard to remark, 'God knows how we'll keep it going for another ten days'. Willie Whitelaw caused some amusement when he accused Labour ministers of 'going about the country stirring up complacency'. (It's often reported, wrongly, that he claimed they were stirring up 'apathy', an even more difficult task, one would imagine, than stirring up 'complacency'.) Meanwhile, Labour's pitch to the public was that they had put an end to the industrial unrest that had blighted Ted Heath's administration. This was true, although it could be argued that they had done so largely by giving in to every demand the unions made.

On election night itself, the first BBC exit poll was

suggesting an overwhelming victory for Labour, with a majority of perhaps as many as 150. However, exit polls then were not nearly as accurate as exit polls now. When the real results started to come in, it was clear that the race was much less clear cut. The BBC rapidly revised its predictions downwards, first to 66 seats and then to 30. Brief elation turned to gloom for Labour supporters as it seemed the gap with the Tories was closing even further. At one point, Wilson, hearing reports that turnout was poor in some traditional Labour areas, despaired. 'We might as well go home,' he is reported to have said at one point. 'We've lost.' He was wrong. They hadn't. A party needed 318 seats to gain a majority. Labour won 319. The Tories had done badly. Heath's party had attracted less than 36 per cent of the national vote and his days as leader were numbered. He had lost three out of the four general elections in which he had been Tory leader. He soldiered grimly on into 1975 but was ousted in a February leadership election by Margaret Thatcher.

Guildford Bombings

On the night of Saturday 5 October, the Provisional IRA targeted two pubs in Guildford because they were both frequented by soldiers from the nearby Pirbright barracks. At approximately 8.50pm, a bomb exploded in the Horse and Groom in North Street, killing five people and injuring dozens of others. Paul Craig, the only civilian among the dead, was a 21-year-old scenic plasterer working at what later became EMI Film Studios. He had joined a group of family and friends, some of them military personnel, one of whom was celebrating her birthday. He was in the wrong place at the wrong time and lost his life as a consequence. So too did Ann Hamilton and Caroline Slater, both teenagers who had enlisted in the Women's Royal Army Corps and only recently begun their basic training. The two other young people who died, 18-year-old William Forsyth and 17-year-old John Hunter, were friends. They were not only both from Barrhead in Renfrewshire but had grown up together in the same street in the town and had joined the Scots Guards together the month before. 'They were just wee lads,' a neighbour told a journalist. 'Why should they be killed? It's madness, absolute madness.'

As a consequence of the blast at the Horse and Groom, other premises in the area were evacuated. Half an hour later, a second device detonated in the Seven Stars. Drinkers had already left the pub but the landlord, Brian O'Brien, suffered a fractured skull and his wife a broken leg. Other members of staff sustained less serious injuries. O'Brien and his barman had just finished searching the Seven Stars but had not found anything suspicious. 'I am sure that the bomb was under a cushion on the bench seats around the bar,' he later said. 'That was the only place we did not look.'

The police were under intense pressure to find the perpetrators of the Guildford bombings. Unfortunately, they chose to take the wrong people into custody and coerced them into confessing to crimes they had not committed. At the end of November, the police arrested the three Irishmen and one Englishwoman – Paul Hill, Gerry Conlon, Paddy Armstrong and Carole Richardson –

who were later to become known as the Guildford Four. A few days later the police raided the house in West Kilburn belonging to Conlon's aunt, Anne Maguire, and also arrested her and a number of other members of her family, including Conlon's father Giuseppe, who had only travelled to London from Belfast after word had reached him of his son's detention. The Guildford Four all retracted their confessions but, in October 1975, were tried, found guilty and sentenced to life imprisonment for the Guildford bombings and, in the cases of Hill and Armstrong, a later pub bombing in Woolwich which had killed two drinkers in the King's Arms on 7 November 1974. The 'Maguire Seven' were charged several months later with possession of explosive materials used in the Guildford bombings and, after conviction, were sentenced to various terms in prison from 4 to 14 years.

It was very quickly clear to some lawyers, journalists and campaigners that the Guildford Four and the Maguire Seven were victims of a terrible miscarriage of justice. The evidence against them consisted of little more than the confessions forced out of the Guildford Four under severe duress and flimsy forensic evidence which appeared to indicate that members of the Maguire family had handled nitroglycerin. Despite the weakness of the prosecution cases and statements from genuine IRA men that exonerated them from involvement in any of the pub bombings, it took years before they were all finally released from prison in 1989 and 1991. For Giuseppe Conlon, it was too late. He died in jail in 1980.

1974

Rumble in the Jungle

Once hyperbolically described by an American journalist as 'arguably the greatest sporting event of the twentieth century', the Rumble in the Jungle was the boxing match which took place in Zaire (now the Democratic Republic of the Congo) between George Foreman and Muhammad Ali on 30 October 1974. Foreman, now perhaps more familiar to younger generations as a salesman of barbecue equipment ('The George Foreman Grill'), was then the undefeated and undisputed heavyweight champion of the world, having beaten Joe Frazier in a bout during which Frazier was knocked down six times in two rounds before the referee stepped in to end the fight. According to one witness, the American writer Norman Mailer, Frazier had looked 'like a man on whom a wall has just fallen'. Foreman was now 25 years old and in peak fitness. He was confident in his own powers. 'I hit a guy and it's like magic,' he said. 'You see him crumbling to the floor. It is a gift from God.'

Ali was considered by many, including himself, as the greatest heavyweight boxer of all time but he was seven years older than Foreman and appeared to be well past his prime. Although he had fought and beaten Joe Frazier earlier in the year (see page 20) for the title of NABF (North American Boxing Federation) Heavyweight champion, many believed that Foreman would have no trouble defeating him. That was the realist's view but Ali appealed to the romantics among boxing fans and those eager to see it as more than just a peculiarly demanding, often brutal sport. 'If ever a fighter had been able to demonstrate that boxing was a twentieth-century art,' Norman Mailer wrote, 'it must be Ali.' There were plenty who agreed with him and harboured the hope that Ali could somehow beat Foreman.

Originally scheduled for 25 September, the fight had to be postponed when Foreman sustained a cut over his eye during a training session. This seemed no more than a minor setback for the champion. He continued to be the runaway favourite. Few believed that Ali could roll back the years and prevail. Dave Anderson, a boxing journalist for the *New York Times*, wrote that, 'sooner or later, the champion will land one of his sledgehammer punches, and for the first time in his career, Muhammad Ali will be counted out'. The well-known sports broadcaster for ABC, Howard Cosell, who was a personal friend of Ali, was nonetheless unconvinced that his pal could emerge victorious. 'I don't think he can beat George Foreman...,' he said on one of his TV shows. 'Maybe he can pull off a miracle. But against George Foreman, so young, so strong, so fearless? Against George Foreman, who does away with his opponents one after another in less than three rounds?' Certainly the champion looked in the mood to make mincemeat of his aging challenger. Norman Mailer, who had flown in to Kinshasa, the capital of Zaire, to witness the spectacle, was in awe when he watched Foreman in training. 'One of the more prodigious sights I've had in my life,' he wrote and noted the 'dents the size of half a watermelon' the boxer made while punching the heavy bag.

Ali was playing his usual game of trying to unsettle his opponent before they stepped into the ring, teasing and tormenting Foreman in press conferences and interviews. A reporter asked the champion if Ali's jibes bothered him. 'No,' Foreman replied. 'He makes me think of a parrot who keeps saying, "You're stupid! You're stupid!" Not to offend Muhammad Ali but he's like that parrot. What he says, he's said before.' When he was asked whether or not he would respond to anything Ali said to him during the fight, he was wryly dismissive of the possibility. 'I never do get a chance to talk much in the ring,' he said. 'By the time I begin to know a fellow, it's all over.'

Once the two men stepped into the ring, Ali was forced to soak up tremendous punishment from the champion for the first few rounds but he had known what was coming and planned for it. He adopted what has come to be known as the 'rope-a-dope' strategy. Norman Mailer, who was at ringside, described it in his own idiosyncratic way. 'The time had come to see if he could outbox Foreman while lying on the ropes,' he wrote. '...He lay back on the ropes in the middle of the second round, and from that position he would work for the rest of the fight, reclining at an angle of ten and twenty degrees from the vertical and sometimes even further, a cramped near-tortured angle from which to box.' The idea was that Foreman would expend all his energy on throwing punches which would land on Ali's arms and body, gaining the champion few points but eventually exhausting him. It worked. By the sixth and seventh rounds, Foreman was visibly tiring. In Mailer's words, his legs had 'the look of a bedridden man who has started on a tour of his room for the first time in a week'. Ali began to taunt his opponent as the two boxers entered clinches. 'Can't you fight harder? That ain't hard,' he muttered in Foreman's ear. 'I thought you was the champion, I thought you had punches.' In the eighth round, Ali summoned up enough strength to land a sequence of punches to which the weary champion had no answer. He stumbled and fell to the canvas. He was able to raise himself to one knee but could not fully haul himself to his feet before the referee signalled the end of the fight. Ali had won a contest in which few had given him much of a chance of victory.

First McDonald's in the UK

Today, when the company has more than 1,200 branches in Britain, it is hard to imagine that there was a time when the Golden Arches of McDonald's were not a familiar sight in the country. However, although the fast-food chain had been established in the USA in the 1940s and the first of its restaurants outside America opened in the 1960s, it was not until October 1974 that the British could enjoy the delights of a Big Mac with fries. And then it was only if they lived in, or were prepared to travel to, Woolwich in south-east London.

Britain was one of the last major European countries to get the benefit of a McDonald's. Not only were property prices comparatively high but the existing competition was well established. Wimpy, another fast food chain which originated in the USA, already had more than 600 restaurants in the UK. McDonald's had initially sought a site in central London for their first venture into the British market but had been unable to find a suitable one. The premises in Woolwich, once a branch of Burtons, the menswear chain, were not ideal but they were inexpensive and the area of south-east London was seen as typical of 'average Britain'. If McDonald's could make a go of it there, then it was likely it could succeed elsewhere as well.

On 12 October, the day of the grand opening, crowds gathered outside, perhaps drawn by the opportunity to meet the Mayor of Woolwich, Len Squirrel, and his chain of office or, more likely, the Radio 1 DJ Ed 'Stewpot' Stewart who was also present. Celebrities of the time continued to visit in the weeks to come. A month later, the boxer Henry Cooper chose the Woolwich McDonald's as the place from which to launch his autobiography. The press was mostly impressed by this new fast food restaurant. The *Daily Mail* praised 'its quintessentially American classlessness', arguing that it was a place 'where minks and mackintoshes could mingle... without any sense of self-consciousness'. Yet, despite the publicity blitz, the restaurant's first manager, a native of Ohio named Paul Preston, later recalled that business was often slow in those first months. 'Nobody knew who we were. We tried every gimmick under the sun – endless free meals and promotions. It took a long while to get going.'

The menu was mostly the standard menu that could be found in McDonald's worldwide. The only concession to British tastes was that, unlike its counterparts in America, the restaurant served tea. The prices now seem remarkably low. A cheeseburger was a mere 21p. Fries were either 10p or 13p, depending on whether you ordered the regular portion or upgraded to a large. The customers on that first day could hand over a 50p coin for a Big Mac and still get 5p back in change. The total takings for that first day were £98. The fast food revolution in Britain had begun.

November

Parts of a hominid skeleton dating back 3 million years
are found in Africa. An English aristocrat disappears
after apparently murdering his children's nanny and
a British MP fakes his own death while staying at a
Miami hotel. The Provisional IRA bomb two pubs
in Birmingham, causing multiple deaths and injuries.
Covent Garden Market moves from the centre of London
after 300 years. In Australia, the first test of the Ashes
series begins with a frightening display of fast bowling.
Humanity sends a message to the stars.

Discovery of 'Lucy'

One of the most significant discoveries to throw light on our remotest human ancestors took place at the Hadar Formation, a site in the Awash Valley in Ethiopia, in 1974. American paleoanthropologist Donald Johanson, then of the Cleveland Museum of Natural History, was one of the leading participants in an international expedition conducting research in the area for a second season. Their first season had produced interesting finds but the second surpassed anything that had so far been discovered. On 24 November, Johanson abandoned his original plan of spending the morning in organising his field notes and instead joined forces with graduate student Tom Gray to scour an area of the site known as Locality 162 for any signs of fossils.

They descended into a little gully which had already been surveyed by other members of the team. As the sun rose higher and the day became ever hotter, it seemed that the pair would be no more successful than their colleagues at finding anything of interest in the gully. They were preparing to leave when Johanson spotted something. 'That's a bit of a hominid arm,' he said to Gray who was not initially convinced that that was what it was. It appeared too small. As the two men stood in the gully debating the nature of their find, they started to see other bits of bone – a femur, vertebrae, part of a pelvis – lying on the ground. It dawned on them that these might all belong to one individual. 'No such skeleton had ever been found,' Johanson later wrote. This was a remarkable discovery. 'We hugged each other, sweaty and smelly, howling and hugging in the heat-shimmering gravel, the small brown remains of what now seemed almost certain to be parts of a single hominid skeleton lying all around us.'

After they returned to report their find, their colleagues were just as thrilled as Gray and Johanson. According to the latter, 'The camp was rocking with excitement'. No one went to bed. A tape of the Beatles song 'Lucy in the Sky With Diamonds' was 'belting out into the night sky', over and over again. Everyone in the camp now travelled to the gully each day for three weeks to collect what could be found. In the end, several hundred pieces of bone were collected which amounted to about 40 per cent of the skeleton of one individual. At some point it was decided that the fossil, definitely that of a female, should be called 'Lucy'. In Amharic, one of the official languages of the country in which it was found, the fossil is 'Dinkinesh' which translates as 'You are Marvellous'. Its scientific but much drabber name is AL 288-1. Lucy, a member of the hominin species *Australopithecus afarensis*, is about 3.2 million years old and remains one of the earliest of our ancestors ever found.

Disappearance of Lord Lucan

At around 9.50pm on 7 November, the handful of drinkers in the Plumbers Arms, a small pub in London's Belgravia, were startled by the sudden arrival of a young woman. She was barefoot and covered in blood. As the barman, Arthur Whitehouse, approached her, she was on the point of collapse. He caught her as she fell and carried her to one of the benches in the bar. An ambulance was called but, before it could arrive, the woman began to cry out. 'Help me, help me, I've just escaped from being murdered,' she shouted, according to Whitehouse. 'My children, my children, he's murdered my nanny.'

At the woman's insistence, police went to 46, Lower Belgrave Street where they were obliged to break down the front door to gain entry. 'I knew there was skulduggery afoot,' Detective-Sergeant Graham Forsyth later said, using curiously archaic language. 'There was blood all over the shop.' A woman's body was found at the bottom of the basement stairs. It was that of Sandra Rivett. She had been nanny to the children of Lady Lucan, the woman whose dishevelled and bloodied appearance had so startled the regulars at the Plumbers Arms. And the leading candidate for the role of murderer in this unfolding drama was Lady Lucan's estranged husband – Richard John Bingham, 7th Earl of Lucan, also 13th Baronet Bingham of Castlebar in County Mayo, Ireland, and 3rd Baron Bingham of Melcombe Bingham in Dorset.

Separated from his wife for nearly two years, Lucan had been in a bitter dispute with her about custody of the children. According to Lady Lucan's account of what happened on the night of 7 November, she had been watching TV in her bedroom with her children and Sandra Rivett. Sandra had, at one point, taken the youngest children to bed and then walked downstairs to make her employer a cup of tea. Time passed and no tea arrived. Lady Lucan went down to the ground floor to investigate. There was no sign of Sandra. Lady Lucan then heard a noise but, before she could work out what it was, somebody leapt from hiding and hit her several times over the head. She screamed and a male voice told her to shut up. She recognised it. It was her husband's. The Lucans then engaged in a violent struggle which ended when she grabbed his testicles. The fight went out of him. 'He desisted,' she later said.

According to Lady Lucan her husband now confessed that he had killed Sandra Rivett, mistaking her in the dark for his real target – his wife. However, he no longer seemed in a murderous mood. He accompanied his wife up the stairs to her bedroom so that they could see what damage he had inflicted on her. At one point, Lucan entered the *en suite* bathroom to get a cloth to clean Veronica's face. 'I heard the taps running,' she told the inquest, 'and I jumped to my feet and ran out of the room and down the stairs.' She exited the house and made her dramatic entry into the Plumbers Arms. Lady Lucan was in no doubt that the intruder and Sandra Rivett's killer was her husband.

As rapidly became clear, he had disappeared. In a letter to a friend, penned in the immediate aftermath of Rivett's death, Lucan wrote that, 'the circumstantial evidence against me is strong... I will lie doggo for a while'. He has, some think, been lying doggo ever since and, although there have been innumerable sightings of him in the last fifty years, he has never been found. Throughout the decades he has been spotted in South Africa, Trinidad, Mexico, Madagascar, Canada, the Philippines and just about every other country in the world. He has been variously reported as working as a waiter in San Francisco, leading the life of an elderly hippy in Goa, playing craps in a gambling joint in Botswana and sleeping in the back of a Land Rover, accompanied by a pet possum, on the outskirts of the small New Zealand town of Marton. He has become less a real man, more a protean figure of myth. The prosaic truth is that Lucan probably committed suicide soon after he disappeared. This was certainly what many of his friends believed. John Aspinall, the gambling impresario and owner of the Clermont Club where Lucan had dined on the night of the murder, thought he had left the country by motor boat en route for the Continent shortly after the killing. In the middle of the English Channel, he had made sure the boat would sink. Then he had tied a weight around his neck and jumped overboard. In his absence, whether dead or in disguise somewhere, he was found guilty of murder by a coroner's jury in June 1975.

Covent Garden Market Closes

Beginning in the 1650s as no more than a few stalls temporarily set up in the grounds of Bedford House, the London home of the Duke of Bedford, Covent Garden Market grew slowly for the next 100 years but, by the end of the eighteenth century, it was the city's best-known fruit and vegetable market. It continued to be so throughout the nineteenth and early twentieth centuries. Henry Mayhew, the Victorian journalist and author of *London Labour and the London Poor*, provided a vivid portrait of the market at its height in the 1850s:

'Nothing is to be seen, on all sides, but vegetables; the pavement is covered with heaps of them waiting to be carted; the flagstones are stained green with the leaves trodden under foot; sieves and sacks full of apples and potatoes, and bundles of broccoli and rhubarb, are left unwatched upon almost every doorstep; the steps of Covent Garden Theatre are covered with fruit and vegetables; the road is blocked up with mountains of cabbages and turnips; and men and women push past with their arms bowed out by the cauliflowers under them, or the red tips of carrots pointing from their crammed aprons...'

In the twentieth century, the problems of the market were at least as noticeable as its liveliness. As early as 1921, the Ministry of Food condemned Covent Garden as 'altogether inadequate to the necessities of the trade' but, in the absence of any better alternative, it continued. By the 1960s, several plans to modernise and rethink the supply of foodstuffs in the capital had been mooted but nothing had happened. It was now even more clear that the area, with its narrow streets and difficulty of access, was no longer suited to the needs of a twentieth-century market. And yet, if the market moved, what was to be done with the Covent Garden piazza? In the late 1960s, the Greater London Council came up with a scheme which would have seen the demolition of most of its distinctive buildings. In response, a Covent Garden Community Association was formed to prevent such monstrous philistinism. The campaign against the GLC's proposals was vigorous and eventually successful. In 1973, the Home Secretary, Robert Carr, designated 250 buildings in the area as listed and any plans to knock down swathes of Covent Garden were abandoned.

Meanwhile, building work to create a new market had begun in 1971 on what had been the Nine Elms

Locomotive Works and the Nine Elms railway station. After more than 300 years, the old market closed on 8 November 1974. Three days later the New Covent Garden Market in Nine Elms opened its doors for the first time. It was inevitable that the old market should go but many people mourned its passing. As the *Times* journalist Philip Howard wrote, 'The centre of London will not be the same without its sweet smell of ripe fruit, its strange vegetable night life, and those midnight lorries roaring in with a breath of the West Country, of Kent, and of the whole wide world'.

Birmingham Pub Bombings

The Provisional IRA continued its bombing campaign in mainland Britain on 21 November with attacks on two pubs in Birmingham. The Mulberry Bush was on the lower two floors of a 25-storey office block in the city centre known as the Rotunda. The first bomb went off there just before 8.20 in the evening, only minutes after a warning of its presence had been given in a call to the *Birmingham Post* newspaper. Ten people were killed and dozens were wounded, many with life-changing injuries. The Tavern in the Town was in New Street, only a short distance from the Mulberry Bush. Drinkers there heard the explosion, 'a muffled thump' according to one, but did not realise what it was. In the wake of the first bombing, police were struggling to clear other venues, including the Tavern in the Town, but a second bomb went off there a mere ten minutes after the one that had devastated the Mulberry

Bush. Like the first it caused deaths and horrendous injuries.

A young man who was in the Tavern in the Town, quoted in a BBC News report, said, 'I was going to put a record on the jukebox when there was an explosion. There were bodies everywhere and I had to clamber over them to get out – the screaming and groaning from the injured was terrifying.' Another witness reported that, 'There were women and young girls screaming, blood pouring everywhere... I saw one man who seemed to have half his body blown off. It was horrible.' A young woman of 20, who had only just arrived at the Tavern a few minutes before, described her own experiences: 'I went over to the bar with my girlfriend, and was just about to buy a drink when there was a bang and everything started falling upon us. I flicked on my lighter and saw my friend next to me had lost her foot. I thought I was also dead and that my spirit was just carrying on, for everywhere I looked there was murder.' Nine people were killed immediately in this second explosion and two died later of their injuries. Every single person in the pub that night was injured in some way, many severely.

Birmingham was traumatised. The Home Secretary, Roy Jenkins, visited the city on the day after the bombings and was aware of 'a pervading atmosphere of stricken, hostile resentment such as I had never previously encountered anywhere in the world'. Anger against Irish people in general was widespread. Some were assaulted in the streets, thrown off buses, refused service in shops and restaurants. (The fact that some of the dead were themselves Irish was conveniently forgotten.) Jenkins was a strong opponent of the death penalty but others in and out of parliament were calling for its reintroduction for such terrorist outrages. A Commons debate revealed the strength of feeling but Jenkins found that leading Tories were of his mind. Willie Whitelaw, for example, argued that all bringing back hanging would do would be to inflame the tensions in Northern Ireland and put British soldiers there in greater danger. In the end, the campaign to restore the death penalty came to nothing. However, four days after the bombings, the 1974 Prevention of Terrorism Act began a swift journey into law. Its powers, Jenkins admitted, were 'draconian'. Indeed, he went on, 'In combination they are unprecedented in peacetime'. However, they were needed. The Act was passed by both Houses of Parliament by 29 November.

During the same period the police moved rapidly to charge six Irishmen, all of them long resident in Birmingham, most of whom had been taken into custody on the selfsame night as the bombings when they were about to take the ferry from Heysham to Belfast in order to attend a funeral. 'We are satisfied that we have found the men primarily responsible,' Assistant Chief Constable Maurice Buck announced. The 'Birmingham Six', as they became known, were put on trial and found guilty of the bombings in August the following year. They were all given life sentences of imprisonment. It was yet another miscarriage of justice to match those of Judith Ward and the Guildford Four (see p. 41 and p. 193) All of the men were entirely innocent but it took until 1991 for the Court of Appeal to quash their convictions.

MP Fakes His Own Death

On 20 November an Englishman staying at the prestigious Fontainebleau Hotel in Miami Beach handed his key to the receptionist and walked down to the hotel's private beach. He was admitted by another hotel employee, undressed to reveal the swimming shorts he had donned earlier and headed for the water, leaving a pile of clothes on the beach. He then swam parallel to the shoreline a short distance, exited the ocean in the grounds of another hotel and made his way to a phone booth where he had already deposited a towel and a fresh set of clothes. Drying himself and changing into his new outfit, he caught a taxi to the airport and retrieved a suitcase, a plane ticket, some cash and a British passport in the name of Joseph Markham from a left luggage office. The Englishman was John Stonehouse, MP for Walsall North, and he had just faked his own death.

Stonehouse was born in Southampton in 1925, the son of a former scullery maid who had become mayor of the city. He joined the Labour Party at the age of sixteen and, after taking a degree at the London School of Economics, he began to look for a path to a political career. After two failed attempts to win a seat in parliament, he was elected MP for Wednesbury in Staffordshire in a 1957 by-election. He was Postmaster General in Harold Wilson's government and then, after that position was abolished in 1969, Minister for Posts and Telecommunication. In many ways, Stonehouse was, throughout the 1960s, the very model of a modern Labour politician, in tune with the zeitgeist, but storm clouds were gathering over his head. In

1969, he was obliged to defend himself against allegations that he was a spy for Czechoslovakia and, although, behind closed doors, he was able to convince Harold Wilson of his innocence, rumours persisted. (It now seems at least a strong possibility that he was indeed an agent for a Warsaw Pact country, although not a very effective one.)

By 1974, and now MP for Walsall North (his Wednesbury consituency had been abolished but he had won a new seat in the February election), Stonehouse faced mounting problems. His finances were in complete disarray. Several companies with which he was involved were either on the brink of bankruptcy or were threatened with what could prove embarrassing investigations by the Department of Trade and Industry. His private life was nearly as complicated. He had long been a serial womaniser. His wife had stoically turned a blind eye to temporary liaisons but what she did not know was that he was now conducting a more serious affair with his secretary, Sheila Buckley, 21 years his junior. As the walls closed in on him, his options seemed limited. He took a flight to Florida and booked into the Fontainebleau Hotel.

The pile of clothes on a Miami beach suggested that he had committed suicide. But had he? Almost immediately, there were doubts that Stonehouse had really drowned. 'People don't believe he's dead,' Tony Benn wrote in his diary only a few days after the news broke. 'They think that with the financial trouble that he's in, he's just disappeared.' The doubters were, of course, completely correct. While Westminster gossips were speculating about his fate, Stonehouse was flitting around the globe on his new Joseph Markham passport. (The name was that of a recently deceased constituent.) After travelling to San Francisco, Hawaii and, briefly, Nouméa in New Caledonia, he arrived in Australia, eventually reaching Melbourne on 27 November, a week after his unconventional checkout from the Fontainebleau Hotel.

His globetrotting was still not over. He now flew to Copenhagen where he met Sheila Buckley and learned how British newspapers were reporting his disappearance. Amidst more sober journalism, wild speculation was rife. One fellow MP, William Molloy, was quoted as suggesting that the Mafia might be involved. 'Terrible though it is to say it,' he told the *Guardian*, 'it is quite on the cards that he has been destroyed by the Mafia.' Quite why the Mafia should be interested in the MP for Walsall was not made clear. Stonehouse now said farewell to his mistress and returned to Melbourne. Back in Australia, his unusual transactions at various banks, carried out under the name of Markham, had aroused the curiosity of the Victoria State Police. Following up on information about odd withdrawals and transfers by a distinguished-looking individual who appeared to have at least two identities (Stonehouse was also using the name Mildoon, another dead man from Walsall), they put the mystery man under surveillance. They briefly considered the possibility that he was Lord Lucan (see p. 206) who had also disappeared in November but word of Stonehouse's alleged suicide had now reached them, as had the speculation that it might have been faked. The Victoria Police contacted Scotland Yard to request pictures of both men.

Photographs arrived and Stonehouse was arrested on Christmas Eve. Any lingering possibility that he might be

Lord Lucan was dismissed when there was no sign on the suspect's body of a large scar the errant peer possessed. Instead, the police were able to identify the man they now had in custody as the absconding MP. However, getting him back to Britain to face the music would be no easy task. After months of legal wrangling, during which Stonehouse attempted to claim asylum in Sweden and then, when the Swedes showed no interest in taking him, in Mauritius, where the government was equally unenthusiastic, he was finally extradited to Britain in July 1975.

He stubbornly refused to resign as an MP and the Labour Party, its minority government needing every parliamentary vote it could get, did not expel him. He continued to appear in Westminster and walk through the division lobbies to cast his vote. In October 1975, Stonehouse gave one of the more extraordinary personal statements ever heard in the House of Commons, occasionally speaking of himself in the third person. He had, he said, been analysed by an eminent psychiatrist in Australia. This person had concluded that the MP had committed 'psychiatric suicide' which 'took the form of the repudiation of the life of Stonehouse because that life had become absolutely intolerable to him'. In an earlier explanation of his behaviour, he had said, 'Lots of MPs go on fact-finding tours overseas. I have been on a fact-finding tour about myself.'

Few people were satisfied by these attempts to exonerate himself and the law now caught up with Stonehouse. He was charged with 21 assorted counts, including fraud, conspiracy to defraud and wasting police time. After a trial at the Old Bailey lasting 68 days, he was convicted and sentenced to seven years in prison. He was released in August 1979, his jail time shortened because of good behaviour. A free man again, Stonehouse took up charity work, joined the SDP, wrote several novels and turned up regularly on TV and radio to discuss his disappearance. His health was poor. He had suffered a number of heart attacks in prison and had undergone open heart surgery. He died on 14 April 1988 after another massive coronary. He was 62 years old. His strange story was brought to the public's attention once more in January 2023 when ITV broadcast a three-part dramatisation of it.

Arecibo Message

Attempts to make contact with alien intelligences via radio waves had begun almost as soon as Marconi had developed the first practicable radio transmitters and receivers at the end of the nineteenth century. In 1901, the maverick genius Nikola Tesla claimed that he had detected a radio signal emanating from Mars, then thought to be, in all likelihood, an inhabited planet. He spent years of his life trying to find a way of establishing a two-way radio communication with the putative Martians.

By 1974, of course, any belief that Mars was inhabited had long since been abandoned by genuine scientists and left to cranks and eccentrics. However, the belief that there must be extraterrestrials out there somewhere in the unimaginable vastness of the universe persisted. Perhaps radio offered a chance to send them word that we existed. Just such a message was despatched from the Arecibo radio telescope in Puerto Rico on 16 November. It was aimed at Messier 13, a globular cluster of many tens of thousands of stars in the constellation Hercules. The cluster was chosen as its destination not only because of the sheer number of stars within it but also because its age, some 11 billion years, suggested that there was a much greater likelihood that an advanced civilisation might have developed there than in younger parts of the universe.

The message was created by the astrophysicist Frank Drake, who was then Director of the US National Astronomy and Ionosphere Center, which included the Arecibo Observatory, with the assistance of the well-known astronomer and TV presenter Carl Sagan. Their aim was to advertise human technological abilities and the extent of our scientific knowledge. The message encoded, in 1679 bits of data, a number of basic scientific facts, including the atomic numbers of certain elements, the double helix structure of DNA and a depiction of the solar system with the Earth highlighted. A stick figure of a human being, our average dimensions and a representation of the number of people on earth were also conveyed.

The message was transmitted for a mere three minutes and it had a very long way to travel. At present, it will have completed about two-thousandths of its total journey, or nearly 300 trillion miles. Because of the vast distances involved, the Arecibo message is expected to reach its destination in about 25,000 years. Whether or not anybody will be there to receive it is another question. In most ways, this scarcely matters. It was never intended as the start of any long-distance conversation over the aeons. 'It was strictly a symbolic event, to show that we could do it,' one of the scientists working at the Arecibo Observatory later said.

In 2001, some 24,983 years before it was expected even to arrive at its destination, an answer to the Arecibo message was received. It came in the form of a crop circle in a field in Hampshire. The reply was an almost exact replica of the original message, except that silicon replaced carbon in the list of chemical elements and the human figure had become a large, bulbous-headed ET. Sadly, the 'Arecibo answer' was almost certainly the work of human astronomers from the nearby Chilbolton radio telescope rather than that of any aliens from the M13 cluster.

First Ashes Test

The first Test Match in a series of six between Australia and the touring MCC team began in Brisbane on 29 November. The tour had begun with a number of drawn matches against state sides but England entered the first Test with some confidence on the back of two victories, against New South Wales and Queensland. This confidence was soon shown to be wildly misplaced. The Brisbane Test was also the first in which what was to become the much-feared fast bowling partnership of Dennis Lillee and Jeff Thomson was noticed. The two men had played together in a single Test against Pakistan two years earlier, which had been Thomson's only cap before this Ashes series, but there had been no signs of future greatness. Indeed Thomson had not taken a single wicket in either of Pakistan's innings. Now their time had come.

Australian captain Ian Chappell won the toss and chose to bat. He and his younger brother Greg both scored fifties as the team made 309, a respectable if not outstanding score on a difficult wicket. Thomson took 3 for 59 in England's first innings, his first test wickets, but was outdone by his fellow fast bowler Max Walker who sent 4 English batsmen back to the pavilion for 73 runs. England ended with 265, Tony Greig making a century. Australia's total of 288 for 5 declared in the second innings left England needing 333 for victory. The stage was set for Thomson. Bowling at tremendous speed, and with terrific venom, he skittled out most of England's top order batsmen, ending with 6 for 46 which were to remain the best bowling figures of his Test career. 'Thomson even frightened me,' former Australian all-rounder Keith Miller commented, 'and I was sitting 200 yards away.'

Over the course of the ensuing Test series, Thomson and Lillee rapidly became bogeymen to English batsmen. 'Ashes to Ashes, dust to dust, if Thomson don't get ya, Lillee must', a caption in an Australian newspaper read. Although it was a major factor in Australian success, their burgeoning partnership was not the only reason that the series finished in February 1975 with Australia victors by four matches to one, with one drawn. This was an Australian team that was filled with excellent players. The Chappell brothers, Ian and Greg, were formidable batsmen, both of whom figure in the all-time top twenty Australian run-makers in Test matches; Rod Marsh was arguably his country's greatest ever wicketkeeper; and Doug Walters was another much-admired batsman who scored more than 5,000 runs in a Test career that lasted

16 years. Mike Denness's England side had its own stars – the veteran batsmen Colin Cowdrey and John Edrich, the wicketkeeper Alan Knott, the all-rounder Tony Greig and the young bowlers, offspinner Derek Underwood and fast bowler Bob Willis – but they all found Lillee and Thomson too hot to handle. 'It was easy to believe,' the cricketing bible, Wisden, recorded, 'that they were the fastest pair ever to have coincided in a cricket team.'

December

The French philosopher and writer Jean-Paul Sartre
pays a much-publicised visit to the imprisoned Andreas
Baader, leader of the Red Army Faction. The last
episode of Monty Python's Flying Circus is broadcast
on BBC 2. In Hollywood, The Godfather II is released.
In Burma, the funeral of former UN Secretary-General
U Thant triggers riots and confrontations between the
government and demonstrators. A man is released from
an Indiana jail after serving 66 years inside. Over the
Christmas holidays, Cyclone Tracy almost completely
destroys the Australian city of Darwin.

Jean-Paul Sartre Visits Andreas Baader

In December 1974, the 69-year-old Frenchman Jean-Paul Sartre was probably the most famous living philosopher. Andreas Baader was one of the world's most notorious urban guerrillas, joint leader of the German far-left terrorist group known as the *Rote Armee Fraktion* (RAF). Indeed the *Rote Armee Fraktion* is often referred to as the Baader-Meinhof Gang. When Sartre announced his decision to visit Baader in the high-security prison of Stammheim near Stuttgart, it was bound to make headlines around the world.

In the 1970s the *Rote Armee Fraktion* was responsible for a series of bomb attacks, kidnappings, bank robberies and politically motivated murders. Andreas Baader was arrested by police after a shootout in Frankfurt in June 1972 and was held in Stammheim awaiting trial. At the time of Sartre's visit more than two years later, Baader and other *Rote Armee Fraktion* prisoners were in the midst of a hunger strike. Indeed, in the previous month, Holger Meins, who had been arrested at the same time as Baader, had starved himself to death. Before his visit, Sartre had been making pronouncements in the press that suggested he was, in some ways, sympathetic to the Baader-Meinhof group which he had described as 'an interesting force' with a 'sense for the revolution'.

The visit itself did not go well. Sartre was prepared to make statements of ambivalent support after it was over. Baader and the other *Rote Armee Fraktion* prisoners were being held in solitary confinement, and thus, according to Sartre, were enduring torture. It was not 'torture like the Nazis', he admitted but it was a kind of torture which would lead to 'psychological disturbance'. (Some people have later suggested that the philosopher who, by this stage in his life, had very poor eyesight, actually mistook the meagrely furnished visitor's room for Baader's cell.) However, Sartre and Baader do not seem to have had a meeting of minds during their hour's conversation. '*Quel con!*', Sartre is reported to have said later. 'What a twat!' Baader dismissed Sartre in secret messages to his fellow prisoners as nothing more than an old man who hadn't understood what he, Baader, was saying. According to an official from the Baden-Würtemmberg State Office of Criminal Investigation, 'During and after the talk, Baader appeared dejected and disappointed that Sartre didn't unreservedly approve of the actions of the Baader-Meinhof Gang'.

In October 1977, Baader and two other members of the *Rote Armee Fraktion* were found dead in their cells at Stammheim. Supposedly they had killed themselves in a suicide pact, although suspicions remain that the full story of their deaths has never emerged and conspiracy theories continue to flourish.

Final Episode of Monty Python's Flying Circus

'This is a party political broadcast,' a voice intones, 'on behalf of the Liberal Party.' What follows is nothing of the sort. Instead, the final episode of the anarchic and hugely influential BBC TV comedy show, *Monty Python's Flying Circus*, begins. The familiar opening sequence from previous series unfolded to the music of John Philip Sousa's march, 'The Liberty Bell', followed by a giant, animated foot, adapted from a painting by the sixteenth-century Italian artist Bronzino, descending from the sky, accompanied by the sound of a whoopee cushion. This was largely ditched in the last series, the first episode of which went out on 31 October 1974. Unlike the previous three series, which had each consisted of 13 episodes, it had only 6. The final one was therefore shown on BBC 2 on 5 December at 9pm.

The Python team had come together five years earlier. Michael Palin and Terry Jones had been at Oxford; John Cleese, Graham Chapman and Eric Idle had studied at Cambridge and all been members of the famous Footlights Club. The troupe was completed by the American animator and future film director Terry Gilliam. After graduating from their respective universities, the English members had all worked as sketch writers and performers in a variety of comedy shows. Cleese, the oldest and probably the best known pre-Python, appeared on *The Frost Report* on BBC1, including in that show's famous 'Class' sketch. Tall and patrician, he had represented the upper-class, looking down his nose at Ronnie Barker's middle-class man and Ronnie Corbett, representative of the working class. Jones, Palin and Idle had all been cast members of *Do Not Adjust Your Set*, a show originally intended for children but which rapidly won an adult audience for its quirky humour. In partnership with Cleese, Chapman had written for comedians such as Roy Hudd and Marty Feldman and he joined him in performing on *At Last the 1948 Show*, another proto-Python sketch show broadcast on ITV in 1967.

In 1969, plans for a new BBC sketch show began to take shape. The Pythons-in-the-making and Ian MacNaughton, who was to direct all but four of the future episodes, met to swap ideas. Various names for the new show were considered, including *Owl Stretching Time*, *The Toad Elevating Moment*, and *Bunn, Wackett, Buzzard, Stubble and Boot*, before they settled on *Monty Python's Flying Circus*. As filming began on the first series, requests to the props department were an early indication of the surreality to come. One asked for a 'copy of Turner's *The Fighting Temeraire*... in a detachable frame which can be broken off and eaten'. Back came a reply that 'all edible props must be obtained through the Catering Manager'.

Broadcast at 10.50 pm on 5 October 1969, the first episode of the new show was watched by an audience of one and a half million. A BBC memo of the time, describing some market research, reveals that it had the approval of 45 per cent of a small focus group of viewers. It didn't necessarily have the approval of senior BBC managers at the time. One privately described it as 'disgusting'; another thought it 'nihilistic and cruel'. Even the controller of BBC 1 was of the opinion, not made public at the time, that the team were 'continually going over the edge of what is acceptable'.

Despite any qualms the BBC panjandrums might have, the audience grew and the show soon went from late-night cult to the most influential comedy of its era. Now legendary sketches, made familiar, perhaps over-familiar, by repetition, put in their first appearances: the Dead Parrot in series 1, the Ministry of Silly Walks and 'Nobody Expects the Spanish Inquisition' in series 2. With the benefit of hindsight, few Monty Python fans would say that the final series had anything to match these classics. John Cleese had left the group by this time, believing that they had done all they could with the sketch-show format. Although material he and Chapman had written was included in it, he was missed. One critic later wrote that 'the physical absence of Cleese is akin to watching the Rolling Stones perform *sans* Mick Jagger'. However, although the TV sketch show was finished, the Monty Python brand of comedy was not. 1975 saw the release of their first wholly original film, *Monty Python and the Holy Grail*. More films followed, most notably *Life of Brian* and *The Meaning of Life*; live shows sold out large arenas; and, over the decades, generations of new fans, many not born when the last series was broadcast, happily continued to recite individual lines and, indeed, entire *Monty Python* sketches to one another.

The U Thant Funeral Crisis

U Thant, former UN Secretary-General between 1961 and 1971, died in New York on 25 November 1974. His body was flown back to what was then Rangoon, the capital of his native Burma (now Myanmar). At the time, as now, the country was ruled by a military junta and there had been no love lost between U Thant and Burma's president, Ne Win. Not only was Ne Win probably envious of the diplomat's worldwide fame and his popularity within Burma, he was also aware that U Thant had been a prominent supporter of the more democratic regime Ne Win had overthrown a dozen years earlier. He therefore refused the late Secretary-

General the honour of a state funeral. Indeed, he decreed that there should be no government involvement in the ceremony at all. This outraged a group of students at Rangoon University for whom U Thant had become a powerful symbol of lost freedoms.

On 5 December, the day of the funeral, U Thant's coffin was taken through streets lined by thousands of mourners to the city's racecourse where it was placed on display before the scheduled burial. At this point, the students seized the coffin and bore it off to the university campus where they held their own alternative ceremony for the deceased. Disagreements between different groups of students, some more radical than others, now arose. The coffin was moved again on 8 December to a site where a temporary mausoleum was under construction. Draped in the UN flag and surrounded by other banners, including the flag of the outlawed students' union, it became the focus for demonstrations against Ne Win's authoritarian government. Speeches were made which were increasingly critical of the regime. It was only a matter of time before the government asserted its power. It closed educational institutions temporarily and shut off communication with the outside world.

Nearly a week after the original kidnapping of the coffin, on 11 December, more than a thousand troops and police attacked the university campus, breaking through the barriers which had been erected around parts of it. They opened fire on students guarding the temporary mausoleum, killing several of them, and took possession of U Thant's body once more. It was taken to be reinterred in the mausoleum U Thant's family had built for it.

Rioting by students and Buddhist monks continued for several days. Buildings were destroyed, cars set on fire and police stations attacked. The government declared martial law. More than 4,000 arrests were made and, amidst more firing by soldiers, more lives were lost.

The Godfather Part II *Released*

The 1970s was a hugely important decade in the history of American cinema, with the continued success of what became known as 'The New Hollywood' and the emergence of major new directors, and 1974 was a significant year. It was a year of great variety. The taste for big, blockbusting disaster movies was at its height. *The Towering Inferno* and *Airport '75* were amongst the Top Ten highest-grossing films of the year. Some veteran directors who had made their name in the 'Golden Era of Hollywood' were still at work. Billy Wilder, for example, released *The Front Page*, a remake of a classic 1930s success, starring Walter Matthau and Jack Lemmon. Other directors with substantial bodies of work behind them had new films out. Sam Peckinpah's *Bring Me the Head of Alfredo Garcia*, Jack Clayton's *The Great Gatsby*, Richard Lester's *Juggernaut*, Sidney Lumet's *Murder on the Orient Express* (with Albert Finney as Hercule Poirot), Richard Fleischer's western *The Spikes Gang*, and Blake Edwards's *The Tamarind Seed* were all released in 1974. Roman Polanski's *Chinatown*, starring Jack Nicholson and Faye Dunaway, was hailed as a neo-noir masterpiece when it hit cinema screens in June.

Comic genius Mel Brooks kickstarted his career with *Blazing Saddles* and *Young Frankenstein*, both of which appeared in the year. *The Texas Chainsaw Massacre*, a cheap, exploitation movie about a family of cannibals, directed by an unknown filmmaker, Tobe Hooper, became an unexpected hit. Two directors who were to go on to better and bigger projects made their directorial debuts, Oliver Stone with a low-budget horror movie entitled *Seizure* and Jonathan Demme with the Roger Corman-produced women-in-prison picture *Caged Heat*. John Carpenter, future director of such horror classics as *Halloween* and *The Thing*, also made his feature film debut in 1974 with the SF comedy *Dark Star*. Michael Cimino, who was to go on to Oscar-winning glory with *The Deer Hunter* and to nearly bankrupt a studio with the massively expensive western *Heaven's Gate*, made his first feature film, *Thunderbolt and Lightfoot*. However, the year's most significant debutant for the future of Hollywood was undoubtedly Steven Spielberg. Three years earlier, he had made a TV movie, *Duel*, which was so impressive that it had gained a theatrical release in many countries but his first feature film was *The Sugarland Express* which appeared on American cinema screens in March 1974.

Most of the big-name directors of New Hollywood had works to their credit in 1974, although not always their most typical. Martin Scorsese's *Alice Doesn't Live Here Anymore* was a gentle comedy, now sandwiched in the director's filmography between the brutal crime stories, *Mean Streets* and *Taxi Driver*; Robert Altman's *Thieves Like Us* adapted a 1930s novel about doomed bank-robbers; Peter Bogdanovich's *Daisy Miller* was a period piece based on a novella by Henry James; Brian De Palma, working with the singer and composer Paul Williams, created his own rock musical version of the 'Phantom of the Opera' story in *Phantom of the Paradise*, a box-office flop at the time but now a cult movie.

In 1974, the New Hollywood director with the highest profile and biggest clout was undoubtedly Francis Ford Coppola. His first contribution to the year's movies was his low-key mystery *The Conversation*, starring Gene Hackman, which was released in April and went on to win the prestigious Palme D'Or at the Cannes Film Festival the following month. His second was *The Godfather Part II*, the sequel to his epic movie starring Marlon Brando as the Mafia capo, Don Vito Corleone, which had appeared on cinema screens two years earlier. The new film told parallel stories in two different time periods. One followed the rise of the young Vito Corleone (Robert De Niro) from poverty in Sicily to the founding of the family firm in 1920s New York; the other featured Al Pacino as Vito's son, Michael, inheritor of his father's power.

On the release of *The Godfather Part II* in December 1974, the critics were divided. The legendary Pauline Kael, not always an easy woman to please, was very impressed. 'The daring of Part II,' she wrote in her review in *The New Yorker*, 'is that it enlarges the scope and deepens the meaning of the first film; *The Godfather* was the greatest gangster picture ever made, and had metaphorical overtones that took it far beyond the gangster genre. In *Part II*, the wider themes are no longer merely implied. The second film shows the consequences of the actions in the first; it's all one movie, in two great big pieces, and it comes together in your head while you watch.' A few years into a career that would later make him the best known film critic in America, Roger

Ebert was not so sure. He thought that there were 'a lot of good scenes and good performances set in the midst of a mass of undisciplined material and handicapped by plot construction that prevents the story from ever really building'. Popular opinion, then and since, has agreed more with Kael than Ebert. *The Godfather Part II* went on to win Best Picture and Best Director, together with four other awards, at the 1975 Oscars. It is now considered one of the greatest American films of all time.

Man Released from Jail After 66 Years

On the morning of 9 December, a prisoner was roused from his bed and told to prepare for his release from Indiana State Penitentiary in Michigan City. Johnson Van Dyke Grigsby, the son of freed slaves, was being paroled for a crime he had committed 67 years earlier in 1907. On 3 December of that year, he was in a bar in Anderson, Illinois, playing poker, when he got into an argument with a white man named James Brown. The argument escalated into a physical fight and Brown threatened Grigsby with a knife. Grigsby left to redeem his own knife from a pawn shop and returned with it to the bar. Brown threw a chair at him whereupon Grigsby lunged at his opponent with the knife, inflicting a wound from which Brown later died. Grigsby claimed that his victim could have saved himself if he had only been sensible. 'He was bleeding, but so drunk he wouldn't see a doctor... Stayed at the bar like a crazy man or something 'stead of gettin' to a hospital. He was a fool, is what he was... Just kept saying, "I don't need no help." We even got a doctor to his house, but he went to bed and didn't want no doctor.' Convicted of second-degree murder, Grigsby was sent to the prison in Indiana, transported there in a horse and cart which took several days to make the journey.

In the decades in which he was imprisoned, he proved a model prisoner, spending much time reading his Bible and an encyclopedia which he called 'an amazing book'. Despite his good behaviour, all of his many applications for parole over the decades were turned down. It was only when he was an old man of 89 that he was told he was finally free to leave. He had been inside for 66 years, 4 months and 1 day. His few possessions consisted of a Bible, a watch, a footspray and a packet of tobacco. Unsurprisingly, Grigsby had become thoroughly institutionalised in the more than 24,000 days he had spent behind bars. After his release, he was unable to cope with life outside the prison walls. Seventeen months later, he was back inside, returning voluntarily. He finally left the penitentiary for good in August 1976. 'I've been here too long,' he is reported to have said. 'I'll not be back.' His new residence was a nursing home in Marion County, Indiana. Other prisoners in the USA have served even longer sentences (Francis Clifford Smith, for example, was incarcerated for just over 70 years before he was finally released in July 2020) but Grigsby's case has become the most famous example of long-term imprisonment. He became sufficiently well-known that Johnny Cash wrote a song, 'Michigan City Howdy Do', about him. Johnson Van Dyke Grigsby died in May 1987, aged 101. 'I've put all my trust in God,' he once said. 'There's got to be a meaning for this.'

Cyclone Tracy Hits Darwin, Australia

One of the worst disasters in twentieth-century Australian history devastated the Northern Territory capital of Darwin in the last month in 1974. The city was hit and very nearly wiped off the map by Cyclone Tracy. As yet unnamed, the cyclone had its origins as weather disturbances in Siberia in early December and these drifted ever southwards. By the 21st of the month, a storm had developed over seas north-east of Cape Don, a lighthouse on the very tip of the Cobourg Peninsula, 225 miles from Darwin. At 10pm that day it was officially designated a tropical cyclone. At that point, Darwin's residents, if they knew of it at all, were untroubled. They had already heard dire predictions about another cyclone, Cyclone Selma, which had earlier been reported as heading in their direction. In the event, it had missed the city. So, when they started hearing about Tracy, many took the news with a pinch of salt. Even Ray Wilkie, who was the Director of the Bureau of Meteorology and had raised an alarm, was concerned early on Christmas Eve that he might be making a mountain out of a molehill. 'I could see on the bunting on the service station, a little bit of wind just moving them. That's how gentle it was.' Everything soon changed. The cyclone struck over the Christmas holidays.

Gusts of wind reached more than 130mph before the instruments measuring them failed. Later estimates by the Bureau of Metereology suggested that, at their height, they passed 150mph. Ships were sunk in the harbour. At the airport dozens of aircraft were either completely destroyed or badly damaged. More than 70 per cent of the city's buildings were destroyed and more than half the population was left homeless. 'Darwin had, for the time being, ceased to exist as a city,' according to leaders of the key emergency services. Estimates of the number of lives lost range from 66 to more than 200.

Eyewitness accounts give some idea of the terror the cyclone brought to the city. 'The noise sticks with you,' remembered Barry Clarke, who was 10 at the time and huddled under his bed in a room filled not only with his own family but with members of two others whose houses had already been destroyed. 'I've never heard wind howl like that since, the rain was just torrential. As it progressed you just kept wondering: when is it going to end? Water started coming around the walls – we found out in the morning that all we had between us and the elements was the ceiling, the roof of the house had gone.'

Another person who was present during the worst of the storm was a 25-year-old British visitor to the city named Ian Cordery. 'I thought I was going to die that night, without doubt,' he told a Sydney reporter decades later. When he looked out at 6.30am on Christmas morning, he could scarcely believe what he was seeing. 'There were no houses. Every home on the street that I lived at the end of was gone.' Now all that was in view was 'street after street of devastation'. In the immediate aftermath of Cyclone Tracy, it seemed as if the city could never recover. 'There's no choice but to evacuate Darwin,' said Alan Stretton, Director-General of the Natural Disasters Organisation. 'There's nothing left to stay for. The city has been almost completely wrecked and the unanimous opinion of the people is that it should be bulldozed and rebuilt.' For a time, the people of Darwin were scattered throughout Australia but there was a determination to bring their city back to life. At a cost of more than $600 million, Darwin was rebuilt from scratch. Today it has a population of 140,000 and is thriving once more.

Bibliography

1974: Scenes From a Year of Crisis is very much popular rather than scholarly history and I have not weighted down the text with footnotes. However, the following bibliography lists books I have consulted while writing it and offers suggestions for further reading to anybody interested in the subjects it (necessarily) covers in brief.

Augar, Philip & Winstone, Keely, *Agent Twister: John Stonehouse and the Scandal That Gripped the Nation*, London: Simon & Schuster, 2022

Barker, Stuart, *Life of Evel*, London: HarperSport, 2010

Beckett, Andy, *When the Lights Went Out: Britain in the Seventies*, London: Faber, 2009

Berg, A Scott, *Goldwyn: A Biography*, London: Hamish Hamilton, 1989

Boatswain, Tim, *A Traveller's History of Cyprus*, Moreton-in-Marsh: Arris Publishing, 2005

Charney, Michael W, *A History of Modern Burma*, Cambridge: Cambridge University Press, 2009

Crouch, Terry, *The World Cup: The Complete History*, London: Aurum, 2002

Cunningham, Sophie, *Warning: The Story of Cyclone Tracy*, Melbourne, Australia: Text Publishing, 2014

DeGroot, Gerard, *The Seventies Unplugged: A Kaleidoscopic*

Look at a Violent Decade, London: Macmillan, 2010

Dheenshaw, Cleve, *The Commonwealth Games: The First Sixty Years 1930-1990*, Victoria, Canada: Orca Books, 1994

Figueiredo, Antonio de, *Portugal: Fifty Years of Dictatorship*, London: Penguin, 1975

Gambaccini, Paul, Rice, Tim, et al, *The Complete Eurovision Song Contest Companion*, London: Pavilion Books, 1998

Graebner, William, *Patty's Got a Gun: Patricia Hearst in 1970s America*, Chicago: University of Chicago Press, 2008

Harper, William T, *Eleven Days in Hell: The 1974 Carrasco Prison Siege at Huntsville, Texas*, Denton, TX: University of North Texas Press, 2004

Hasse, John, *Beyond Category: The Life and Genius of Duke Ellington*, New York: Simon & Schuster, 1993

Hayes, Julian, *Stonehouse: Cabinet Minister, Fraudster, Spy*, London: Robinson, 2021

Hitt, David, Garriott, Owen and Kerwin, Joe, *Homesteading Space: The Skylab Story*, Lincoln, Nebraska: University of Nebraska Press, 2008

Hoffer, Richard, *Bouts of Mania: Ali, Frazier and Foreman and an America on the Ropes*, London: Aurum, 2014

Johanson, Donald C & Edey, Maitland A, *Lucy: The Beginnings of Humankind*, London: Granada Publishing, 1981

Kapuscinski, Ryszard, *The Emperor: Downfall of an Autocrat*, San Diego: Harcourt Brace Jovanovich, 1983

Mailer, Norman, *The Fight*, London: Little, Brown, 1975

Man, John, *The Terracotta Army: China's First Emperor and the Birth of a Nation*, London: Bantam Press, 2007

BIBLIOGRAPHY

Marcus, Harold G, *A History of Ethiopia: Updated Edition*, Berkeley CA: University of California Press, 2002

McGladdery, Gary, *The Provisional IRA in England: The Bombing Campaign 1973-1997*, Dublin: Irish Academic Press, 2006

McKinstry, Leo, *Sir Alf: A Major Reappraisal of the Life and Times of England's Greatest Football Manager*, London: HarperSport, 2006

Oliver, Brian, *The Commonwealth Games: Extraordinary Stories behind the Medals*, London: Bloomsbury, 2014

Pedahzur, Ami, *The Israeli Secret Services and the Struggle Against Terrorism*, New York: Columbia University Press, 2009

Rolls, Albert, *Stephen King: A Biography*, Westport, Connecticut: Greenwood Press, 2009

Sandbrook, Dominic, *Seasons in the Sun: The Battle for Britain 1974-1979*, London: Allen Lane, 2012

Sandbrook, Dominic, *State of Emergency: The Way We Were: Britain 1970-1974*, London: Allen Lane, 2010

Sounes, Howard, *Seventies: The Sights, Sounds and Ideas of a Brilliant Decade*, London: Simon & Schuster, 2006

Thomas, Clem & Thomas, Greg, *125 Years of the British and Irish Lions: The Official History*, Edinburgh: Mainstream Publishing, 2013

Thompson, Laura, *A Different Class of Murder: The Story of Lord Lucan*, London: Head of Zeus, 2014

Toobin, Jeffrey, *American Heiress: The Wild Saga of the Kidnapping, Crimes and Trial of Patty Hearst*, London: Profile Books, 2017

True, Everett, *Hey Ho Let's Go: The Story of the Ramones*, London: Omnibus Press, 2002

1974

Turner, Alwyn W, *Crisis? What Crisis?: Britain in the 1970s*, London: Aurum Press, 2008

Werth, Barry, *31 Days: The Crisis That Gave Us the Government We Have Today*, New York: Doubleday, 2006

Wheen, Francis, *Strange Days Indeed: The Golden Age of Paranoia*, London: Fourth Estate, 2009

Acknowledgements

My thanks should first of all go to my publisher Ion Mills who encouraged me to advance in time to write this follow-up to my earlier book, *1922*. I would also like to thank all of Ion's colleagues at Oldcastle Books whose friendliness and professionalism make dealing with the company such a pleasure: Ellie Lavender, who was always on hand with help and advice; Lisa Gooding; Sarah Stewart-Smith; and Demi Echezona. Jayne Lewis and Steven Mair once again used their exceptional copy-editing and proofreading skills to pick up the mistakes in my original manuscript; any that remain are my responsibility. Elsa Mathern produced a very striking cover for the book, as she did for *1922*.

As always, friends and family have provided encouragement during the months I was researching and writing *1974*. Love and thanks to my sister, Cindy Rennison, to my mother, Eileen Rennison, and to my German family, Wolfgang, Lorna and Milena Lüers. In a series of phone calls, my great friend, David Jones, came up with many excellent ideas for subjects to include in the book, and it is dedicated to him. Other friends who either kindly suggested *1974* topics or listened patiently, on the phone or in person, as I rambled on about the events of that year, are: John and Karen Magrath, Hugh Pemberton, Susan Osborne, Richard and Jane Monks, Dr

Kevin Chappell, Anita Diaz, Travis Elborough, Andrew Holgate, and Graham Eagland. My thanks to all of them. Thanks should also go to Heather, Marcus, Hettie, David, Caitlin, Debs, Liam, Liv, Leah, Harrison, Joe, Amber and all the other staff (sorry I can't name check everybody) at the Funky Monkey in Davenport, the friendliest coffee shop in Greater Manchester, who, on most days, kept me appropriately topped up with caffeine during the writing of this book. In writing *1974*, as in all the work I do, my biggest debt is to my wife Eve whose love, support and encouragement are ever present.

Index

INDEX

Also Available from Oldcastle Books

oldcastlebooks.co.uk/1922

1922 was a year of great turbulence and upheaval. Its events reverberated throughout the rest of the twentieth century and still affect us today, more than 100 years later.

Empires fell. The Ottoman Empire collapsed after more than six centuries. The British Empire had reached its greatest extent but its heyday was over. The Irish Free State was declared and demands for independence in India grew. New nations and new politics came into existence. The Soviet Union was officially created and Mussolini's Italy became the first Fascist state.

In the USA, Prohibition was at its height. The Hollywood film industry, although rocked by a series of scandals, continued to grow. A new mass medium – radio – was making its presence felt and, in Britain, the BBC was founded. In literature it was the year of peak modernism. Both T. S. Eliot's *The Waste Land* and James Joyce's *Ulysses* were first published in full.

In society, already changed by the trauma of war and pandemic, the morals of the past seemed increasingly outmoded; new ways of behaving were making their appearance. The Roaring Twenties had begun to roar and the Jazz Age had arrived.

In a sequence of vividly written sketches, Nick Rennison conjures up all the drama and diversity of an extraordinary year.

'This is a delightful book, and Rennison's selection is intelligent and lively. He has an eye for the significant detail and an agreeably dry tone... *1922* should please those who are well-versed in history, but it will also be a treat for those for whom the past is another country' – *Scotsman*

◉LDCASTLE BOOKS

POSSIBLY THE UK'S SMALLEST
INDEPENDENT PUBLISHING GROUP

Oldcastle Books is an independent publishing company formed in 1985 dedicated to providing an eclectic range of titles with a nod to the popular culture of the day.

Imprints include our lists about the film industry, KAMERA BOOKS & CREATIVE ESSENTIALS. We have dabbled in the classics, with PULP! THE CLASSICS, taken a punt on gambling books with HIGH STAKES, provided in-depth overviews with POCKET ESSENTIALS and covered a wide range in the eponymous OLDCASTLE BOOKS list. Most recently we have welcomed two new sister imprints with THE CRIME & MYSTERY CLUB and VERVE, home to great, original, page-turning fiction.

oldcastlebooks.com

 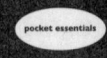 kamera BOOKS **creative** ESSENTIALS  cmc

OLDCASTLE BOOKS	CREATIVE ESSENTIALS	THE CRIME & MYSTERY CLUB
POCKET ESSENTIALS	PULP! THE CLASSICS	VERVE BOOKS
KAMERA BOOKS	HIGHSTAKES PUBLISHING	